The
Official Rules of
Basketball

TRIUMPH
BOOKS
CHICAGO

The National Collegiate Athletic Association
6201 College Boulevard
Overland Park, KS 66211-2422

This cover and design treatment © Triumph Books.
Cover photo courtesy of Brian Spurlock.
Typography: Sue Knopf.
Cover design by Patti Frey.
Referee and player icon design by Mark Anderson Design, Chicago.

This book is available in bulk at special discounts for your group or
organization. For further information, contact:

Triumph Books
601 South LaSalle Street
Chicago, Illinois 60605
(312) 939-3330
(312) 663-3557 (fax)

ISBN 1-57243-428-7

Printed in Canada

Contents

User's Guide

This edition of the Official Rules of NCAA Basketball has been designed to give basketball fans of all ages a quick and easy reference guide to the action on the court.

A good place to start is in the Index (arranged by key word), where you'll find references to all the rulings on a given subject in one place.

This edition contains the following material:
Official NCAA Men's and Women's Basketball Rules; and Official Basketball Rules Interpretations.

New rules or changes in the rules for 2002 are indicated by shading, as shown with this paragraph.

The Interpretations are examples of game situations that illustrate how the Rules are applied. Interpretations are indicated by a special icon, as shown in the margin of this paragraph.

Headings at the top of left-hand pages refer to the Rule under discussion; right-hand headings refer to the particular Section under discussion on that page.

Rule 1

Court and
Equipment

Rule 1

Court and Equipment

Section 1. **The Game**

Art. 1. Basketball is played by two teams of five players each. The objective is for each team to throw or tap the ball into its own basket and to prevent the other team from scoring.

Art. 2. The ball may be thrown, batted, rolled or dribbled in any direction, subject to the restrictions that follow.

Section 2. **The Playing Court—Dimensions**

Art. 1. The playing court shall be a rectangular surface free from obstructions with sidelines of 94 feet in length and end lines of 50 feet in length.

Art. 2. The court dimensions shall be marked as shown on the court diagram.

Section 3. **Lines and Other Markings**

Art. 1. The court shall be marked with boundary lines (sidelines and end lines) and other lines and markings as shown on the court diagram.

Art. 2. Instead of the 2-inch boundaries listed on the diagram, it is legal to use contrasting-colored floor areas by painting the out-of-bounds area, the center circle, and the free-thow lanes and lines so that the mathematical line between the two colors is the boundary. Such a contrasting-colored out-of-bounds belt should be at least 8 inches wide.

Art. 3. The restraining line shall be a color that is different from that of the end lines. Non-playing personnel shall not be permitted in this area.

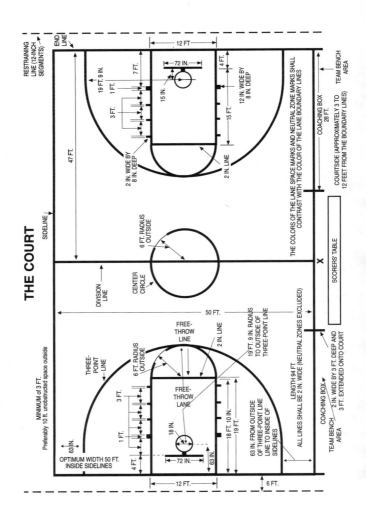

Art. 4. A shadow line is a line that designates the required 2-inch width by use of border or outline lines at least ¼ -inch wide, which shall lie within the 2-inch width.

Art. 5. When the floor has a logo on the playing court, that logo should not distract from the visibility of the division line or center-circle line.

Section 4.   Center Circle

Art. 1. When a logo distracts from the visibility of the 2-inch center-circle line as shown on the court diagram, one of the following shall be permissible:

a. Solid 2-inch wide interrupted line; 4 inches long, 2-inch break; 4 inches long, 2-inch break, etc.
b. Shadow-bordered 2-inch wide line (¼-inch borders).
c. 2-inch wide interrupted shadow line: 4 inches, 2-inch break, 4 inches, 2-inch break, etc.
d. ¼-inch single-bordered line (radius of 6 feet to the outside edge).
e. Mathematical line formed by contrasting-colored floor areas.

Art. 2. The unmarked spaces for the non-jumpers around the center circle shall be 36 inches deep.

Section 5.   Division Line

Art. 1. The division line shall divide the playing court into two equal parts and shall be formed by extending the center-circle diameter in both directions until it intersects the sidelines.

Art. 2. Instead of the solid 2-inch line as shown on the court diagram, the following shall be permissible:

a. A solid 2-inch wide interrupted line; 4 inches, 2-inch break, 4 inches, 2-inch break, etc.
b. Shadow-bordered 2-inch wide line (¼-inch borders)
c. Interrupted 2-inch wide shadow line: 4 inches, 2-inch break, 4 inches, 2-inch break, etc.

Section 6.   **Free-Throw Lane**
Art. 1. All lines designating the free-throw lane, but not lane-space marks and blocks, are part of the lane.
Art. 2. The color of the lane-space marks and blocks shall contrast with the color of the lane boundary lines.
Art. 3. The area of the free-throw lane inside the boundary lines shall be one color.
Art. 4. The lane-space marks and blocks shall identify areas that extend 36 inches from the outer edge of the lane lines toward the sidelines.

Section 7.   **Three-Point Field-Goal Line**
Art. 1. The three-point field-goal lines shall be the same color as the free-throw lane boundary lines and the semicircles.

Section 8.   **Coaching Box**
Art. 1. The coaching boxes shall extend from the sideline to the back of the team benches.
Art. 2. The coaching-box lines shall contrast in color with that of the sidelines and end lines.

Section 9.   **Backboards—Dimensions, Materials**
Art. 1. Each backboard shall be marked as listed on the backboard diagram.
Art. 2. The size of the backboards may be either of two dimensions:
a. 6 feet horizontally and 3½ feet vertically; or
b. 6 feet horizontally and 4 feet vertically.
Note: The 6 feet horizontal and 3½ feet vertical dimensions are recommended for replacement backboards or new installations.
Art. 3. The backboards shall be similar in size at both ends of the playing court.
Art. 4. A transparent, rigid, rectangular backboard, with a flat surface shall be used.
Art. 5. Backboards shall not be tinted.

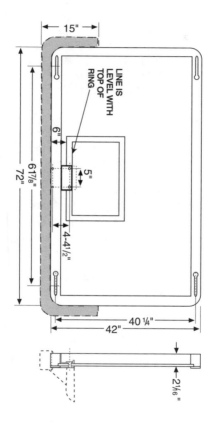

Section 10.   Backboards—Padding

Art. 1. The padding shall be a single solid color and shall be the same color on both backboards.

a. When it becomes necessary to use a substitute backboard, the padding shall be of the same color as that of the backboard being replaced.

Art. 2. The padding shall be 1-inch thick from the front and back surfaces of the backboards.

Art. 3. The material shall be 2 inches from the bottom edge of each backboard.

Art. 4. The padding shall cover the bottom surface of each backboard and the side surface to a distance of 15 inches up from the bottom. The front and back surface must be covered to a minimum distance of 3/4 inch from the bottom of each backboard.

Section 11.   Backboards—Support Systems

Art. 1. Padding—Any backboard support behind a backboard and at a height of less than 9 feet above the floor shall be padded on the bottom surface to a distance of 2 feet from the face of the backboard. All portable backstops shall have the bases padded to a height of 7 feet on the court-side surface.

Art. 2. Protrusions and Clearances

a. Protrusions below backboards shall not be allowed.

b. Any backboard support, all of which is not directly behind the backboard, shall be at least 6 inches behind the backboard when the support extends above the top and at least 2 feet behind the backboard when the support extends beyond the side.

c. Any support system below or behind a backboard shall be at least 8 feet behind the plane of the backboard face and a height of 7 feet or more above the floor.

Section 12. **Backboards—Positions**

Art. 1. Each backboard shall be midway between each sideline, with the plane of its front face perpendicular to the floor, parallel to and 4 feet from each end line.

Art. 2. The upper edge of each backboard shall be 13 feet above the floor.

Art. 3. Each backboard shall be protected from spectators to a distance of at least 3 feet at each end.

Art. 4. Portable backboards shall be secured to the floor to prevent movement.

Section 13. **Baskets—Size, Material**

Art. 1. Each basket shall consist of a single metal ring, 18 inches inside diameter, its flange and braces, and a white-cord, 12-mesh net, 15 to 18 inches in length, suspended from beneath the ring.

Art. 2. Each ring shall measure not more than ⅝ inch in diameter, with the possible addition of small-gauge loops on the under-edge for attaching a 12-mesh net. Each ring and its attaching flange and braces shall be bright orange in color.

Art. 3. The cord of each net shall be not less than 120-thread nor more than 144-thread twine, or plastic material of comparable dimensions, and constructed so as to check the ball momentarily as it passes through.

Section 14. **Baskets—Ring**

Art. 1. Each basket ring shall be securely attached to each backboard/support system with a ring-restraining device. Such a device will ensure that the basket stays attached, even when a glass backboard breaks.

Art. 2. The upper edge of each basket ring shall lie 10 feet above and parallel to the floor and shall be equidistant from the vertical edges of that backboard. The nearest point of the inside edge of each ring shall lie 6 inches from the plane of the face of that backboard.

Art. 3. Both movable and non-movable rings are legal.

Section 15.   The Ball

Art. 1. The ball shall be spherical.

Art. 2. The ball's color shall be the approved orange shade.

Art. 3. The ball shall have a deeply pebbled leather cover unless both teams agree to use a ball with a non-leather cover.

Art. 4. The ball shall have the traditionally shaped eight panels, bonded tightly to the rubber carcass.

Art. 5. The width of the black rubber rib (channels and/or seams) shall not exceed 1/4 inch.

Art. 6. When dribbled vertically, without rotation, the ball shall return directly to the dribbler's hand.

Art. 7. The air pressure that will give the required reaction shall be stamped on the ball. The ball shall be inflated to an air pressure such that when it is dropped to the playing surface from a height of 6 feet measured to the bottom of the ball, it will rebound to a height, measured to the top of the ball:

a. (**Men**) of not less than 49 inches when it strikes its least resilient spot nor more than 54 inches when it strikes its most resilient spot.

b. (**Women**) of not less than 51 inches when it strikes its least resilient spot nor more than 56 inches when it strikes its most resilient spot.

Art. 8.

a. (**Men**) The circumference of the ball shall be within a maximum of 30 inches and a minimum of 29½ inches.

b. (**Women**) The circumference of the ball shall be within a maximum of 29 inches and a minimum of 28½ inches.

Art. 9.

a. (**Men**) The weight of the ball shall not be less than 20 ounces nor more than 22 ounces.

b. (**Women**) The weight of the ball shall not be less than 18 ounces nor more than 20 ounces.

Art. 10. The home team shall provide a ball that meets the specifications listed in this Section. The referee shall judge the legality of the ball and may select for use a ball provided by the visiting team when the home team cannot provide a legal ball.

Note: It is recommended that the home team provide the visiting team with warm-up balls of the same type as the game ball.

INTERPRETATION

Play: Visiting team B's captain notices that Team B's pregame warm-up balls are of a different type than the official game ball. Team B's coach requests that Team B be allowed to warm up using the type of ball to be used in the game.

Ruling: The official shall inform Team A's game management that Team B shall be allowed to warm up with the same type of ball(s) that will be used during the game.

Section 16. Logos/Names/Equipment

Art. 1. Logos, names or equipment of any kind (including school and conference logos or names, cameras and microphones) shall not be permitted on the backboards, rings and padding around the backboards, or on or attached to the shot clocks.

Art. 2. The manufacturer's name and/or logo shall be permitted on the ball.

Art. 3. An institution's name or logo shall be permitted on the ball.

Art. 4. There are no restrictions on team or conference logos, names or abbreviations on the playing court, provided they do not obscure any of the required lines. (See Rule 10-3.8.)

Art. 5. Commercial logos shall be permitted on the playing court when they conform to the following standards:

a. The logo(s) shall fit into a box that is 10 feet by 10 feet square;

b. This box shall be located 8½ feet from the division line and 4½ feet from the sideline;

c. Logo(s) shall be within the two 10 feet by 10 feet squares, with no more than one square in each half of the playing court.

Note: See Rules 3-5.8 and 3-6 for logos and labels on players' equipment.

Section 17.   Scoreboard, Game-Clock Display

Art. 1. A visible game clock shall be required.

Art. 2. An alternate timing device and scoring display shall be available in the event of malfunctions.

Art. 3. Division I schools shall have a game clock that shows a 10th-of-a-second display when less than one minute remains in a period. It is highly recommended that Division II schools have a game clock that shows a tenth-of-a-second display when less than one minute remains in a period.

Note: Division I schools shall comply with this rule by the 2002-03 season. The Division II recommendation is effective for 2003-04 season. Division III schools are exempt from this requirement and recommendation but are permitted to have such equipment.

Art. 4. Division I schools shall have a red warning light placed behind each backboard to indicate when the period-ending horn has sounded. It is highly recommended that Division II schools have a red warning light placed behind each backboard to indicate when the period-ending horn has sounded.

> **Note:** *Division I schools shall comply with this rule by the 2002-03 season. The Division II recommendation is effective for the 2003-04 season. Division III schools are exempt from this requirement and recommendation but are permitted to have such equipment.*

Section 18. Shot-Clock Displays

Art. 1. Two visible shot clocks shall be mandatory.

Art. 2. An alternate timing device shall be available in the event a visible shot clock malfunctions.

> **Art. 3.** A shot clock shall be recessed and mounted behind each backboard.
>
> **Note:** *Division I schools shall comply with this rule by the 2002-03 season. Division II shall comply by 2003-04. Division III schools are exempt from this requirement but are permitted to have such equipment.*

Art. 4. When it is not possible to recess the shot clocks, when possible, they shall be mounted on the wall and positioned to the left of each basket as viewed from the center of the playing court.

Art. 5. When it is not possible to recess or mount the shot clocks on the wall, they shall, as a last resort, be located on the floor at each end of the playing court so that they are visible to players and the shot-clock operator.

Section 19. Possession Indicator

Art. 1. A visible display located at the scorers' table shall be available to indicate team possession in the alternating process.

Section 20. Team Benches—Scorers' and Timers' Table

Art. 1. Choice of benches is made by the home-team game administration.

Art. 2. The team benches shall be located equidistant from the division line extended at each side of the scorers' and timers' table on the sidelines.

Art. 3. The scorers' and timers' table shall be located court-side and at mid-court.

Art. 4. Teams shall warm up at the end of the playing court farthest from their own bench for the first half.

INTERPRETATION

Play: The visiting team is advised that its team bench is located (a) farther from the division line than the home team's or (b) on the opposite end line from the home team's.

Ruling: Game shall be played with benches as located by home-team management. The referee has no authority to move the location of either bench unless for player safety; however, mutual consent should have been obtained before the game. (See Preface.)

Rule 2

Officials and
Their Duties

Rule 2

Officials and Their Duties

Section 1. **The Officials**

Art. 1. The officials shall be:

a. A referee and an umpire; or a referee and two umpires;

b. Two timers, two scorers and a shot-clock operator, who shall assist the referee and umpire(s). A single timer and single scorer may be used when they are trained personnel acceptable to the referee.

Art. 2. The officials' uniform shall be a black-and-white striped shirt and black pants.

Art. 3. The scorers, timers and shot-clock operator shall be located at the scorers' table at court-side.

Section 2. **Officials' Authority**

Art. 1. The officials shall conduct the game in accordance with the official rules and interpretations and employ the mechanics of officiating outlined in the NCAA-approved men's or women's basketball officiating manuals.

Art. 2. No official has the authority to set aside any official rules or approved interpretations.

Art. 3. No official shall have authority to set aside or question decisions made by the other official(s) within the limits of their respective outlined duties.

Art. 4. One official may assist another by providing additional information related to a made decision.

Art. 5. The referee's decision shall not take precedence over that of the umpire(s) in calling a foul or violation.

Section 3.   Elastic Power

Art. 1. The referee shall be empowered to make decisions on any points not specifically covered in the rules.

Section 4.   Officials' Jurisdiction

Art. 1. The officials shall have the power to make decisions for infractions of rules committed either within or outside the boundary lines from 30 minutes (**men**) and 15 minutes (**women**) before the scheduled starting time of the game through the referee's approval of the final score.

Art. 2. For **men**, at least one official shall arrive on the floor 30 minutes before the start of the game.

Art. 3. For **women**, officials may leave the court after the 10-minute mark during pregame and return by the three-minute mark.

Art. 4. When the referee leaves the confines of the playing area at the end of the game, the referee's jurisdiction has ended and the score has been approved. (See **women's** approval of score in officiating guidelines in the Appendix.)

INTERPRETATIONS:

Play 1: Team A is ahead by one point. The game-ending horn sounds with the ball loose at the division line. Clearly after playing time has expired, A1 jumps and smacks the backboard. The referee, who is near the free-throw line, on his or her way to the scorers' table to check/approve the final score, sees this action by A1 and assesses an indirect technical foul. Team A's coach pushes the referee after the indirect technical foul is called. The referee ejects the coach and awards Team B three free throws.

Ruling: The referee is correct. The officials' jurisdiction does not end until the approval of the final score. Until the officials' jurisdiction ends, an official may call a technical foul, correct a correctable error (Rule 2-10), or correct a bookkeeping mistake by the official scorer.

Play 2: In the same situation as in A.R. 1, a school official is sitting in the bleachers with a camcorder. May the official consult the camcorder?
Ruling: No. A camcorder that is not at a court-side table is not a court-side monitor; however, if the camcorder and all necessary equipment were on an official court-side table, the camcorder could be consulted.

Play 3: In the same situation as in A.R. 1, a team manager is filming the team video from an elevated position. The official requests that the manager bring the tape to the scorers' table so that the official can play it in the videocassette player and television that are on the scorers' table. Is this legal?
Ruling: No. The entire unit, including the tape, must be at a court-side table. If the tape had been filmed from the court-side table and the videocassette player and television were on that table, it would have been legal to consult the tape.

Play 4: The officials leave the playing area and while they are in the locker room, it is discovered that there is a mistake in the score or that there was a request for a correctable error (Rule 2-10).
Ruling: When the officials leave the playing area, the score has been approved and the game is over.

Section 5. Officials' Use of Replay/Television Equipment
Art. 1. Officials may use court-side replay equipment, videotape or television monitoring only in situations

involved in preventing or rectifying a scoring or timing mistake or malfunctioning game clocks or shot clocks, to determine if a fight occurred and those individuals who participated in a fight, or to assess whether correctable errors 2-10.1.c, d, or e need to be rectified.

Art. 2. At the end of the second half or at the end of any extra period, the officials shall use replay equipment, videotape or television monitoring that is located on a designated court-side table (i.e., within approximately 3 to 12 feet of the playing court), when such equipment is available, to ascertain whether a try for field goal that will determine the outcome of a game (win, lose, tie), and is attempted at or near the expiration of the game clock, was released before the sounding of the period-ending horn.

INTERPRETATION

Play: A1 releases a try for goal near or at the expiration of time for the game. The official rules the field goal to be a successful two-point goal. Before an official goes to a court-side monitor to confirm the status of the play, the coach from Team A requests a correctable error on the grounds that the goal was counted erroneously and three points should have been awarded.

Ruling: It shall be permissible for the officials to use the court-side monitor to determine if a goal has been counted erroneously. The officials shall notify the coaches of both teams of their intention to use the court-side monitor for this purpose. When the coach's appeal is ruled to be incorrect, a 75-second timeout in games not involving electronic media or either a 60- or 30-second timeout in games involving electronic media shall be charged to his or her team. When that timeout excedes the allotted number, an indirect technical foul shall be assessed. The officials shall be required to use the court-side monitor to ascertain whether a try for field goal that is game-deciding or will determine whether there is an(other) extra period was taken at or near the expiration of the game clock was released before or after the sounding of the game-clock horn.

Art. 3. Officials shall be permitted to consult a court-side monitor to determine if a try for goal is a two- or three-point attempt, regardless of whether the try is successful.

Art. 4. Officials shall not use a court-side monitor or court-side videotape for judgment calls such as who fouled, basket interference, goaltending or release of the ball before the sounding of the horn, with the exception of the situations described in Rules 2-5.2 and 2-5.3.

Section 6. The Referee—Pregame Duties

Before the game starts, the referee shall:
Art. 1. Inspect and approve all players' uniforms, all equipment, including playing court, baskets, ball, backboards, and timers'/scorers' signals.
Art. 2. Designate the official clocks and timers/operators.
Art. 3. Designate the official scorebook and official scorer.
Art. 4. Assure that the official timer will be responsible for notifying each team three minutes before each half is to begin.
Art. 5. Notify the captains when play is about to begin at the start of the game.

Section 7.   The Referee—Duties During Game

During the game, the referee shall:

Art. 1. Toss the ball in the center circle for jump balls to start the game and any extra period(s).

Art. 2. Administer the alternating-possession arrow to start the second half.

Art. 3. Decide whether a goal will count when the officials disagree.

INTERPRETATION

Play: One official observes traveling, stepping out of bounds or another violation by A1. At approximately the same time, A1 tries for a field goal and another official observes contact by B1.
Ruling: The officials shall decide which act occurred first. There is nothing inherent in such acts to make it necessary to rule them as occurring simultaneously. When the violation occurred first, the ball became dead. When the ball was in flight during the try before the traveling or the touching of the boundary line, there was no violation. When the contact occurs after a violation is observed, it shall not be a foul unless an unsporting factor was involved.

Art. 4. Forfeit the game when the conditions warrant.

Art. 5. Decide matters upon which the timers and scorers disagree.

Art. 6. Inform each team and the table officials of the overtime procedures when the score is tied at the end of regulation time.

Art. 7. Correct a scoring or bookkeeping mistake.

Art. 8. Check the score of each half and extra period(s) and approve the final score.

Section 8.   Officials' Duties

During the game, officials shall:

Art. 1. Put the ball in play.

Art. 2. Determine when the ball becomes dead.

Art. 3. Prohibit practice during a dead ball, except between halves.

Art. 4. Administer penalties.

Art. 5. Grant and charge timeouts.

Art. 6. Beckon substitutes to enter the playing court.

Art. 7. Indicate a three-point attempt and signal a successful three-point goal.

Art. 8. (**Men**) Silently and visibly count seconds to administer throw-in, free-throw, back-court, and closely guarded rules and silently count for adjudication of the three-second rule.

Art. 9. (**Women**) Silently count seconds to administer the free-throw and three-seconds rules and visibly count seconds to administer the throw-in and closely guarded (when holding the ball) rules.

Art. 10. Notify the captains when play is about to begin after an intermission or a timeout.

Art. 11. Report a warning for delay to the official scorer and coaches.

Art. 12. Signal the official timer to stop the game clock when a foul occurs, designate the offender to the official scorer and indicate with finger(s) the number of free throws.

Art. 13. Clearly signal, when a team is entitled to a throw-in:

a. The act that caused the ball to become dead.

b. The team entitled to the throw-in.

c. The designated spot, unless the throw-in comes after a successful goal or an awarded goal.

Section 9. **Officials' Duties Related to Conduct**

The officials shall:

Art. 1. Penalize unsporting conduct by a player, coach, substitute, team attendant or follower.

INTERPRETATIONS

Play 1: Who is responsible for behavior of spectators?

Ruling: The home management or game committee, insofar as it reasonably can be expected to control the spectators, is responsible. The officials may call fouls on either team when its supporters act in such a way as to interfere with the proper conduct of the game.

Play 2: After a foul is called against a home team player, just before the free-thrower releases the ball, he/she is hit by a coin thrown by a spectator.

Ruling: Assess an indirect technical foul against the home team, award the visiting team two free throws and put the ball in play at the point of interruption. (See Rule 10-3.7).

Art. 2. Penalize flagrant misconduct by any offender.

Art. 3. Remove a player from the game who commits his or her fifth foul.

Art. 4. Notify the coach and then the player when there is a disqualification.

Section 10. **Correctable Errors**

Art. 1. The correctable errors are listed in this section. In order to correct any of them, such errors must be recognized by an official during the first dead ball after the game clock has been started properly.

a. Failing to award a merited free throw.

INTERPRETATIONS

Play 1: B1 pushes A1 during an unsuccessful try. A1 is awarded two free throws. The first free throw by A1 is successful, after which B2 takes the ball out of bounds under Team A's basket and passes to B3, who passes to B4 for an uncontested field goal in Team B's basket. The captain of Team A then calls to the attention of an official that A1 did not receive a second free throw.

Ruling: The goal by B4 shall count. A1 shall be permitted to attempt the second free throw with no players lined up along the free-throw lane. The ball shall then be awarded to Team A out of bounds at the end line nearer Team B's basket and the thrower-in shall be permitted to run the end line. This was the point where the game was stopped to correct the error.

Play 2: After the bonus is in effect, B1 holds A1. A1 erroneously is not awarded a bonus. A1 is awarded the ball out of bounds and completes the throw-in to A2. The coach of Team A notifies the official scorer that the coach wants to meet with the official concerning a correctable error. When Team A scores a field goal, the official scorer sounds the game-clock horn and advises the official of the coach's request for the conference. The official recognizes the correctable error after talking with the coach and official scorer.

Ruling: The field goal by Team A shall count. This error is correctable because it happened within the prescribed time limit of Rule 2-10.2. A1 shall be awarded his or her merited free throw(s).

Play 3: B1 fouls A1 after the bonus is in effect. A1 is not awarded the bonus free throws. Team A shall be awarded the throw-in. Team A controls the ball inbounds, and A3 eventually asks for and receives a timeout. During the timeout, an official recognizes the correctable error or it is called to his or her attention that A1 should have been awarded a one-and-one free-throw attempt(s).

Ruling: A1 shall be awarded the one-and-one and play shall be resumed as after any normal free throw(s).

b. Awarding an unmerited free throw.

INTERPRETATIONS

Play 1: Before the bonus rule is in effect, B1 fouls A1. The official errs by awarding A1 a one-and-one attempt. (a) A1 makes the first free-throw try, and the error is then discovered; or (b) A1 is successful in both free-throw attempts and then the official detects the error; or (c) A1 misses the front end of the one-and-one and the game clock starts, at which time the official detects the error; or (d) A1 is successful in the first bonus attempt but misses the second free-throw try and, as a result, the game clock starts and B1 scores a field goal. In each of the four situations, the error shall be called to the attention of the official before the first dead ball becomes live after the game clock starts.

Ruling: Each of the four situations is a correctable error. In (a), (b), and (c), Team A shall be awarded the ball at the designated spot. In (d), Team A shall be awarded the ball out of bounds at Team B's end line, which was the point of interruption, to correct the error. Any free throws made in any of the four situations shall be canceled.

Play 2: After a one-and-one is shot by Team A and during the first dead ball after the game clock was started off the missed free throw, the coach of Team B states that Team A was not in the bonus and should not have shot the one-and-one. The official finds that Team A was indeed in the bonus and charges Team B with a timeout. Team B does not have any timeouts left.

Ruling: **(Men)** Team B shall be charged with an indirect technical foul. Any player from Team A will shoot two free throws with the lane cleared and the ball shall be put back in play at the point of interruption. (Women) Team B shall be charged with an indirect technical foul. Any player from Team A will shoot two free throws with the lane cleared and the ball shall be awarded to the offended team at the point of interruption.

Play 3: B1 fouls A1 and Team A is not in the bonus. The official erroneously awards A1 a one-and-one free throw. A1 is successful on the first try; but misses the second and B1 rebounds the ball. B1 dribbles down the floor and scores a field goal. The official is called to the bench by the coach of Team B who points out that A1 erroneously had been awarded a one-and-one.

Rulng: The official shall order the official scorer to cancel A1's successful free throw. The ball shall be awarded to Team A for a throw-in from the end line by B's basket, which was the point of interruption.

Play 4: B1 fouls A1 and it is Team B's ninth foul of the second half. The official erroneously awards A1 two free throws instead of a one-and-one. A1 (a) makes two free throws, or (b) misses the first free throw and makes the second free throw, or (c) misses both free throws. Within the correctable-error time limitations, the officials shall be notified of their error.

Ruling: In (a), A1 was entitled to the second free throw because the first free throw was successful. Both free throws shall count, and play shall be resumed at the point of interruption. In (b), A1's first free throw, to which he or she was entitled as the first part of a one-and-one, was unsuccessful and the player should not have been awarded a second free throw. The successful second free throw shall be nullified, and play shall be resumed at the point of interruption. In (c), A1's unmerited second free throw was unsuccessful, so it shall be ignored, and play shall be resumed at the point of interruption.

c. Permitting a wrong player to attempt a free throw.

INTERPRETATION

Play: A1 is fouled by B1 during a field-goal attempt and the try is successful. A2 erroneously is awarded the free throw. While A2's successful attempt is in the air: (a) B1 fouls A3, or (b) B1 intentionally fouls A3. Before the ball becomes live, the coach of Team B properly asks the referee to correct the error of awarding the free throw to the wrong player.

Ruling: The free throw by A2 shall be canceled; and A1 shall properly attempt the free throw. The common foul by B1 in (a) shall be canceled. The intentional foul in (b) cannot be canceled. The error shall be corrected when A1 is given the free throw to which A1 was entitled as a result of the original foul. In (b) the game shall continue with the administration of the two free throws to A3 resulting from the intentional foul by B1. Team A shall be awarded the ball at the designated spot.

d. Permitting a player to attempt a free throw at the wrong basket.

e. Erroneously counting or canceling a score.

INTERPRETATIONS

Play 1: (a) A1, or (b) B1 is called for basket interference at Team A's basket. In (a), the referee erroneously counts the score or, in (b), erroneously fails to count the score. In each case, the error is discovered before the first dead ball has become live after the game clock has started.

Ruling: The official's error in both (a) and (b) shall be correctable because the error was recognized within the proper time limit.

Play 2: Team A has the ball and is working for a shot. The shot-clock horn sounds and then A1 shoots and scores an apparent field goal. The shot-clock horn is not heard by the officials on the playing court. Play continues with Team B inbounding the ball. With 20 seconds remaining on the shot clock, the official calls traveling on B1. At that time, the official timer calls the referee to the scorers' table to explain that the shot clock had sounded before A1 scored the field goal.

Ruling: The basket shall be canceled because the error was made while the game clock was running. The official has until the second live ball after the error to make the correction. The error shall be correctable until the ball is put in play after the traveling call.

Art. 2. When the officials' error in Rule 2-10 is made while the game clock is running and the ball is dead, it must be recognized by an official before the second live ball to be correctable.

Art. 3. When the error is a free throw by the wrong player, a free throw attempted at the wrong basket or the awarding of an unmerited free throw, the free throw and the activity during it, other than a flagrant misconduct technical foul, an intentional technical foul or an indirect or direct technical foul, shall be canceled.

a. Points scored, time consumed and additional activity, which may occur before the recognition of the error, shall not be nullified.

Art. 4. When an error is corrected, play shall be resumed from the point at which it was interrupted to correct the error, unless the correction involves awarding merited free throw(s) and there has been no change of team possession since the error was made. In that case, play shall resume as after any normal free throw.

Section 11. Duties of Scorers

The scorers shall:

Art. 1. Record the field goals made and the free throws made and missed, and shall keep a running summary of the points scored.

Art. 2. Record the personal and technical fouls called on each player and notify an official immediately when the fifth foul, including any combination of personal fouls, direct technical fouls and intentional technical fouls; or the third technical foul is charged to a squad member or bench personnel.

INTERPRETATIONS

Play 1: B1 commits a fifth foul (any combination of personal fouls, direct technical fouls and intentional fouls), which results in two free throws for A1. The official scorer and official timer fail to notify either of the game officials that a fifth foul has been committed. When the scorers realize the mistake, they inform the official timer to sound the game-clock horn. The official timer sounds the device as the first free throw is made or missed. The referee asks the scorers' table personnel to explain the problem. The referee is advised that B1 has committed five fouls, after which the referee advises the coach and player of Team B that B1 has five fouls. The coach replaces B1. Shall any free throw be awarded to Team A?

Ruling: No. This is a bookkeeping mistake for which B1 shall not be held responsible; no penalty shall be assessed.

Play 2: A player who has committed a fifth foul (any combination of personal fouls, direct technical fouls and intentional technical fouls) continues to play because the scorers have failed to notify the officials.

Ruling: As soon as the scorers discover the irregularity, they should sound the game-clock horn after (or as soon as) the ball is in control of the offending team or is dead. The disqualified player shall be removed immediately. Any points that may have been scored while such a player was illegally in the game shall count. When other aspects of the error are correctable, such as permitting the wrong player to attempt a free throw, see Rule 2-10.

Art. 3. Notify an official immediately when a second direct technical foul is charged to a coach, squad member or any bench personnel.

Art. 4. Notify an official immediately when a combination of any three technical fouls has been assessed or when three bench direct technical fouls have been called on a team.

Art. 5. Record any ejection for fighting.

Art. 6. Record the timeouts charged to each team and notify a team and its head coach, through an official, when such team takes its final allowable charged timeout.

Art. 7. Signal the nearest official each time a team is granted a charged timeout in excess of the allowable number.

Art. 8. Signal the nearest official in each half when a player commits a common foul (except a player-control foul), beginning with the team's seventh foul and the team's 10th foul, including any combination of personal fouls, direct technical fouls, intentional technical fouls and flagrant technical fouls.

Art. 9. Designate that the scorebook of the home team shall be the official scorebook, unless the referee rules otherwise. The official scorebook shall remain at the scorers' table throughout the game, including all intermissions.

INTERPRETATIONS

Play: At halftime, the official scorer, who is a member of the home-team faculty, removes the scorebook from the scorers' table: (a) of his or her own volition; or (b) at the request of the home team coach.

Ruling: In (a), when the removal is inadvertent and momentary, there should be no penalty. When there is evidence that the official scorer removed the scorebook to take it to the home-team dressing room, an indirect technical foul shall be assessed to the home team. In (b), when the home-team coach requests the official scorer to remove the scorebook, the home team shall be assessed a direct technical foul.

Art. 10. Compare their records after each goal, each foul and each charged timeout, notifying the referee at once of any discrepancy. When no error can be found, the referee shall accept the record of the official scorebook, unless the referee has knowledge that permits another decision. When the discrepancy is in the score and the error is not resolved, the referee shall accept the progressive team totals of the official scorebook.

Art. 11. Correct a scoring or bookkeeping mistake any time before the referee approves the final score.

INTERPRETATIONS

Play 1: The official scorer fails to record two points awarded to Team A by an official during the first half as a result of basket interference by B2.
Ruling: The bookkeeping mistake shall be rectified.

Play 2: After two minutes of the first extra period, it is discovered that during the second half of regulation play, the official scorer failed to record one point as a result of a made free throw by Team A.
Ruling: The score shall be recorded and play shall be continued at a designated spot from the point of interruption.

Art. 12. Keep a record of the names and uniform numbers of players who are to start the game and of all substitutes who enter the game.

a. It is recommended that squad members' names be entered in the scorebook in numerical order.

Art. 13. Notify the nearest official when there is an infraction of the rules pertaining to submission of the roster, substitutions or uniform numbers of players.

Art. 14. When necessary, signal the officials with a sounding device unlike that used by the referee and umpire(s). This sounding device may be used immediately when (or as soon as) the ball is dead or is in control of the offending team.

INTERPRETATION

Play: The game-clock horn sounds while the ball is live.

Ruling: Players should ignore the game-clock horn since it does not cause a dead ball. The officials shall use their judgment in blowing the ball dead to consult with the scorers and timers. When the players do not ignore the game-clock horn and stop playing, the officials shall award the ball to the team in control at the designated spot.

Art. 15. When a correctable error is called to the official scorer's attention by a coach while the game clock is running, the timer shall not use the game-clock horn until the ball has become dead.

Art. 16. For ease of identifying the official scorer, an X or an NCAA logo shall be placed on the floor in front of the individual's spot at the scorers' table. When an X is used, it shall be composed of 12-inch line segments that are 2 inches in width. When an NCAA logo is used, it shall be a minimum of approximately 8 inches in diameter.

Note: It is recommended that only the person at the scorers' table permitted to wear a black-and-white-striped garment be the official scorer and that he or she be seated next to the official timer.

Section 12. Duties of Timer

The official timer shall:

Art. 1. Be provided with a game clock to be used for timing periods and intermissions and a stopwatch for timing timeouts. The game clock and stopwatch shall be placed so that they may be seen by both the timer and the shot-clock operator.

Art. 2. Operate the game clock.

Art. 3. Note and notify the referee more than three minutes before each half is to start.

Art. 4. Signal the scorers three minutes before starting time.

Art. 5. Record playing time and time of stoppages.

Art. 6. Start the game clock as prescribed in Rule 5-9.

INTERPRETATION

Play: (**Men**) The game clock indicates that 1:13 is left in the second half when Team A makes a throw-in after a charged timeout. Team A is charged with a 10-second back-court violation, but the game clock shows that only eight seconds were used. The official timer indicates that the game clock started when the throw-in was touched on the playing court.

Ruling: Violation. Team B shall be awarded a throw-in at a designated spot. Rule 2-10 does not provide for the correction of an error made in the referee's counting of seconds.

Art. 7. Start the stopwatch for a charged timeout and signal the referee when it is time to resume play.

Art. 8. Sound a warning signal 15 seconds before the expiration of the 30-second time limit to replace a disqualified player. The signal also shall be sounded at the end of the 30 seconds to replace a disqualified player.

Art. 9. Sound a warning signal 15 seconds before the expiration of an intermission or charged timeout. A second signal shall be given at the expiration of an intermission or a charged timeout. Play shall be resumed immediately upon the sounding of the second signal.

INTERPRETATION

Play: The official timer properly sounds a warning signal 15 seconds before a charged timeout expires and a final signal when the timeout ends. The official administering the throw-in sounds the whistle to alert the players that the game shall resume; however, neither team has left its huddle on the sideline. *Ruling:* The official shall award the ball at a designated spot and begin the throw-in count. (See Rule 9-4.1.d.)

Art. 10. Stop the game clock at the expiration of time for each period and when an official signals a timeout.

INTERPRETATION

Play: As the official calls a five-second closely guarded violation, the official sounds the whistle and gives the signal to stop the game clock. The official sees the exact time remaining in the second half while doing this. The game clock shows five seconds remaining. The game clock shall be stopped; (a) at five seconds; or (b) at not more than four seconds; or (c) at three seconds; or (d) the time runs out completely. *Ruling:* In (a), there has been no obvious timing mistake. However, in (b), (c) and (d), more than one second has elapsed from the time that the signal was given until the timing device was stopped. The referee shall order five seconds to be put on the game clock. In all cases listed in this A.R., the referee has definite information that the game clock showed five seconds and shall instruct the official timer to put that time on the game clock.

Art. 11. Stop the game clock after a successful field goal with 59.9 seconds or less remaining in the game or any extra period with no substitution allowed during the dead-ball period.

Art. 12. Indicate with the game-clock horn the expiration of playing time in each half or extra period. This signal shall terminate player activity.

Art. 13. Enter the playing court or use other means to immediately notify the referee when the timers' signal fails to sound or is inaudible. When, in the meantime, a goal has been made or a foul has occurred, the referee shall consult the timers.

a. When the timers agree that time expired before a try for field goal was in flight, the goal shall not count.

b. When the timers agree that the period ended (as in Rule 5-7.2.c) before a foul occurred, the foul shall be disregarded unless it was intentional or flagrant.

c. When the timers disagree about the expiration of time before a successful try for field goal or foul, the goal shall count or the foul shall be penalized unless the referee has knowledge that alters such a ruling.

INTERPRETATION

Play: In a game with no official court-side television monitor, the signal to end the last period cannot be heard. The officials disagree whether the ball was in flight during a try for field goal or whether a foul occurred before time expired.

Ruling: The final decision shall be made by the referee. The official timer shall indicate if the ball was in flight before the game-clock horn sounded only when requested to do so by the referee. The referee shall use his or her best judgment; but when the evidence for counting or not counting the goal or foul is equal, the referee shall rule that the goal counts. In a game with an official court-side television monitor, the status of the try for goal shall be ascertained with the use of the court-side monitor; however, the court-side monitor shall not be used to determine whether a foul was committed before the time expired.

Art. 14. When an obvious error by the official timer has occurred because of the failure to start or stop the game clock properly, the error may be corrected only when the referee has definite information relative to the time involved.

Section 13.   Duties of Shot-Clock Operator

The shot-clock operator shall:

Art. 1. Use a 35-second shot clock for men and a 30-second shot clock for **women**.

Art. 2. Use the shot clock for the entire game, including extra periods, except when 35 seconds or less (**men**) or 30 seconds or less (**women**) remain in the half or extra period, in which case the shot clock shall be turned off.

Art. 3. Control a separate timing device with a horn that shall have a sound that is distinct and different from that of the game-clock horn.

Art. 4. Have an alternate timing device available.

Art. 5. Start the timing device when a player inbounds legally touches or is touched by the ball on a throw-in or when a team initially gains possession from a jump ball, an unsuccessful try for goal or a loose ball.

Art. 6. Stop the timing device and reset it:

a. When team control is re-established after the team loses possession of the ball;

b. When a foul occurs (***Exceptions:*** Rules 2-13.7.e, .f and .g);

c. When a held ball occurs (***Exceptions:*** Rule 2-13.7.d and 2-13.7.g);

d. When a try for goal strikes the ring or flange; or

e. When a violation occurs.

Note: *The mere touching of the ball by an opponent does not start a new shot-clock period when the same team remains in control of the ball.*

INTERPRETATION

Play: A1 touches the ball that was thrown-in by A2. The ball strikes the playing court and bounces until A3 gains control by dribbling. The shot-clock operator started the shot clock when A1 touched the ball.

Ruling: The operator was correct. Touching the ball initiates the start of the game clock in all cases and the shot clock when there is more than 35 seconds left in the period (**men**) or more than 30 seconds left in the period (**women**).

Art. 7. Stop the timing device and continue time without a reset when play begins under the following circumstances:

a. The ball is deflected out of bounds by a defensive player;

b. A player is injured or loses a contact lens;

c. A charged timeout has concluded; and

d. During team control as defined in Rule 4-13, a defensive player causes a held ball and the alternating-possession arrow favors the offensive team.

e. After a double personal foul when there is team control as defined in Rule 4-13 and as described in Rule 7-4.1.h.

f. After a double personal foul when a team is in possession of the ball for a throw-in as described in Rule 7-4.1.h.

g. After any technical foul is assessed to the team in control of the ball or to the team in possession of the ball during a throw-in or to bench personnel or followers of that team, when these conditions exist.

> ***Exceptions:*** A single intentional technical foul or a single flagrant technical foul.

h. After a simultaneous held ball as described in Rule 7-4.1.g occurs during a throw-in and the alternating-possession arrow favors the throw-in team.

Note: *The offensive team, upon regaining possession of the ball for the throw-in, shall have the unexpired time on the shot clock to attempt a try.*

INTERPRETATION

Play: A1 releases the ball on a try for goal, B1 partially blocks the shot and the ball (a) hits the ring or flange; (b) goes out of bounds; or (c) goes through the basket.

Ruling: In (a) and (c), the play is legal and the action shall continue. In (b), the official shall blow the whistle to stop play and the shot-clock operator shall stop but not reset the shot clock. On the ensuing throw-in by Team A, the game clock and shot clock shall start when the throw-in touches any player on the playing court.

Art. 8. Sound the shot-clock horn at the expiration of the shot-clock period. This shot-clock horn shall not stop play unless recognized by an official's whistle. When the shot clock indicates :00 but the shot-clock horn has not sounded, the shot-clock time has not expired.

Art. 9. The shot clock shall be turned off when the game clock shows less time than a shot-clock period.

INTERPRETATIONS

Play 1: An official inadvertently blows the whistle and the shot-clock horn sounds while the ball, after being shot by A1, is in the air. How is play resumed when the shot (a) is successful or (b) does not strike the ring or flange or (c) strikes the ring or flange but does not enter the basket?

Ruling: In (a), the whistle and shot-clock horn shall be ignored. In (b) and (c) play shall be resumed by the alternating-possession procedure and the shot clock shall be reset to the full shot-clock period.

Play 2: There are 37 seconds (**men**) or 32 seconds (**women**) on the game clock and 35 seconds (**men**) or 30 seconds (**women**) on the shot clock. Team A uses time before A1 releases the ball for a try for goal. After A1 releases the ball, the shot-clock horn sounds. The ball does not strike the ring or flange. The officials call a shot-clock violation. At the same time as the official's whistle, the game clock sounds, signaling that the period has ended. Shall the official put two seconds back on the game clock?

Ruling: No. The shot-clock horn sounded at the expiration of the shot-clock period; however, this does not stop play unless recognized by the official's whistle. The official's whistle for the shot-clock violation stopped play. The expiration of playing time was indicated by the timer's signal. This signal shall terminate player activity (Rule 2-12.12). The period ended with the violation.

Art. 10. Allow the timing device to continue during a loose-ball situation when the offense retains possession or when a field-goal try is attempted at the wrong basket.

Art. 11. Allow the game officials to make the final decision when there is doubt as to whether a score was made within the shot-clock period or whether a try for goal contacted the ring or flange.

Rule 3

Players, Substitutes and Player Equipment

Rule 3

Players, Substitutes and Player Equipment

Section 1.   **The Team**

Art. 1. At the start of the game, each team shall consist of five players, one of whom shall be the captain.

INTERPRETATION

Play: Teams A and B each have co-captains. At the pregame conference, one of the co-captains requests permission from the referee that both co-captains be allowed to confer with officials on interpretations.
Ruling: Co-captains may participate in the pregame conference, but only one co-captain of each team may confer with the officials during the game. During the pregame conference, the referee shall be informed which co-captain of each team shall be the speaking co-captain during the game.

Art. 2. Each team may continue to play with fewer than five players when all other squad members are not eligible or able to play.

Art. 3. When there is only one player participating for a team, that team shall forfeit unless the referee believes that both teams have an opportunity to win.

Section 2.   **The Captain**

Art. 1. The captain is the representative of the team and may address an official on matters of interpretation or to obtain essential information, when it is done in a courteous manner. Dialogue between coaches and officials should be kept to a minimum.

Art. 2. Any player may address an official to request a timeout or permission to leave the playing court.

Section 3. **Lineup**

Art. 1. Before the 10-minute mark is reached on the game clock that is counting down the time before the start of the game, each team shall supply the scorers with:

a. Names and uniform numbers of squad members who may participate, and those of the five starting players.

INTERPRETATION

Play: Nine minutes before the scheduled starting time for the game, Team A presents its squad roster and its starting lineup to the official scorer and then, at six minutes before the game's starting time, Team A presents four additional names to the official scorer for the squad list.

Ruling: Team A shall be assessed one indirect technical foul and the game shall start with a jump ball.

Art. 2. After the time limits specified have been reached, a team shall be charged with a maximum of one indirect technical foul for one or more of the following:

a. Failure to comply with Rule 3-3.1.

b. Adding name(s) to the squad list.

c. Changing squad member's number(s) without reporting the change(s) to the scorers and an official.

INTERPRETATION

Play: Team A properly submits its squad list and designates its five starters in compliance with the rule before the starting time of the game. However, the uniform number for each squad member is erroneously indicated. The mistake is not detected until approximately 1½ minutes have been played.

Ruling: An indirect technical foul shall be charged to Team A. A player shall wear the uniform number indicated in the scorebook or the scorebook number shall be changed to that which he or she is wearing. When the squad member, before participating, changes the uniform number he or she wears to that indicated in the scorebook, there shall be no penalty. When the number in the scorebook for a player is changed before participation and the change is reported to both the official scorer and an official, there shall be no penalty.

d. Changes in the starting lineup, except when the changes are necessitated by obvious injury or illness, or to replace a designated starter to shoot a technical-foul free throw.

INTERPRETATION

Play: A1, who is designated as a starter 10 minutes before the scheduled starting time of the game, becomes ill one minute before the game is to start.

Ruling: A1 may be replaced without an indirect technical foul being assessed. Illness or injury is considered to be an extenuating and unavoidable circumstance that permits a substitution without penalty. A1 shall be permitted to enter the game later if able.

Art. 3. Once the game begins, a team can be charged with a maximum of one indirect technical foul for the infractions listed in Articles 1 and 2 of this section.

Section 4.   Substitutions

Art. 1. Each substitute who desires to enter the game shall give the scorers his or her uniform number.

Art. 2. Substitutions between halves shall be reported to the official scorer by the substitute(s) or a team representative before the signal that ends the intermission.

Art. 3. Substitutions during a timeout must report to or be in position to report to the official scorer before the warning signal. Substitutions shall not be permitted after the warning signal.

INTERPRETATION

Play: After the second warning signal sounds after a timeout, A1 goes to the free-throw line to attempt two free throws. Before the first free throw, A6 reports to the official scorer and tries to enter the game as a substitute.

Ruling: A6 cannot enter the game because the second warning signal has sounded and there has been no live ball followed by a dead-ball sequence.

Art. 4. When entry is at any time other than between halves, and a substitute who is entitled and ready to enter reports to the scorers, the timers shall sound the horn when (or as soon as) the ball is dead and time is out.

Art. 5. Substitutions shall not be permitted after successful field goals in the last minute of the game and the last minute of any extra period.

INTERPRETATION

Play: After a successful field goal with 48 seconds left on the game clock, the timer sounds the game-clock horn for substitute A6 to enter the game.

Ruling: A6 shall not be permitted to enter. The rule states that while the game clock is stopped after successful field goals in the last minutes of play, substitutions shall not be allowed. A team may request a timeout and then insert substitutions any time the ball is dead and the game clock is stopped.

Art. 6. Any substitute shall remain outside the boundary line until beckoned by an official, whereupon the substitute shall enter immediately. When the ball is about to become live, the beckoning signal should be withheld.

INTERPRETATION

Play: After a successful free throw, A1 enters the playing court before the throw-in, and A1's illegal entry is not detected until after the ball becomes live.

Ruling: A1 became a legal player when the ball became live. Because discovery of the infraction came after the ball becoming live, the infraction by A1 shall be ignored. (See Rule 10-3.5.a.)

Art. 7. An entering player shall not replace a free-thrower or designated jumper. When the substitute desires to replace a player who is to attempt a free throw, the substitute shall remain at the scorers' table until the next opportunity to enter the game.

Art. 8. During multiple free-throw personal fouls, a substitute may enter the game only before the final attempt in the sequence unless otherwise authorized by the rules or after the final attempt has been successfully converted.

Art. 9. (Women) When a player is required to be replaced, such as for disqualification, injury or blood, before the administering of multiple free throws, then all other substitutes who legally reported to the official scorer before the player had to be replaced may enter the game.

INTERPRETATIONS

Play 1: A1 is fouled and his or her try for goal is unsuccessful. During the try: (a) B1 commits his or her fifth (disqualifying) foul against A1; (b) A3 is injured or is bleeding, has blood on his or her body, or his or her uniform is saturated with blood and he or she cannot continue to play; (c) A4 is wearing illegal apparel.

Ruling: (**Men**) In all cases, a substitute shall be allowed into the game to become a player before the last try of the mutiple free throw. No other substitutions shall be allowed.

Ruling: (**Women**) In all cases, a substitute shall be allowed into the game to become a player before the last try of the mutiple free throw. In addition, all substitutes who had legally reported before the player had to be replaced may enter the game.

Play 2: After the second warning signal sounds for a timeout, A1 goes to the free-throw line to attempt two free throws. After the first free throw is successful and before the ball is at the disposal of A1 for the second free throw, A6 reports to the official scorer to become a substitute and then tries to enter the game as a substitute.

Ruling: A6 shall be allowed to enter before the last attempt of the multiple personal foul free throw because a live ball followed by a dead ball has occurred.

Art. 10. A player who has been replaced by a substitute may re-enter the game at the next opportunity to substitute, provided that the game clock has been properly started with his or her replacement in the game.

Art. 11. A player who has been withdrawn may re-enter the game at the next opportunity to substitute, provided that the game clock has been properly started with his or her replacement in the game.

INTERPRETATIONS

Play 1: A direct technical foul is assessed against Team A. B6 replaces B1 and makes the second free throw. After the attempt, B1 desires to re-enter.
Ruling: Illegal. B1 may not re-enter before the next opportunity to substitute after the game clock has started after his or her replacement.

Play 2: During a dead ball, A6 replaces A5. Before the ball is put into play, a direct or indirect technical foul is assessed against Team B. A5 is designated by the coach to enter the game and attempt the free throw(s) resulting from Team B's technical foul.
Ruling: A5 may not re-enter to attempt the free throw(s) because the game clock has not been started since A5 left the game.

Art. 12. A player who legally enters the game during a dead ball may leave the game during that same dead-ball period without penalty.

INTERPRETATION

Play: A1 is injured during a play in which A1 was fouled. As a result, A1 cannot attempt the free throw awarded to him or her. A6 replaces A1 and attempts the free throw, which is successful. A7 replaces A6 before the game clock starts.
Ruling: The procedure is legal. (See Rule 8-2.2.a.)

Art. 13. A player who has been injured to the extent that the coach or any other bench personnel is beckoned and/or comes on to the playing court shall be directed to leave the playing court once the extent of the injury has been ascertained unless a timeout is requested by his or her team.

INTERPRETATION

Play: A1 is injured and the referee beckons the coach and/or athletic trainer onto the playing court to assist the injured player. Before the injured player is replaced, Team B requests and is granted a time-out. Play is about to resume and A1 is back on the playing court.

Ruling: A1 shall be prohibited from staying on the playing court. Team B's timeout does not make A1 eligible to return to play. Team A must request and be granted a charged timeout in order for A1 to remain in the game.

Art. 14. When three or more substitutes for the same team enter the game, an official may honor a request by the captain of the opposing team to aid it in locating the entering players.

Section 5.   Uniforms

Art. 1. The torso of the game jersey shall be a single solid color from the base of the neck to the bottom of the game jersey. There shall be no color restrictions in the area of the game jersey from the base of the neckline to the shoulder seam. (When a back shoulder panel is used, it shall extend no more than 3 inches from the shoulder seam and shall be of the same color/design as the panel on the front of the game jersey from the base of the neckline to the shoulder seam.)

Art. 2. Game jerseys shall be tucked in the game pants. *Note: The first time an official must tell a player to tuck in the game jersey, the official shall issue a warning to the head coach. The next time any player on the same team has the game jersey untucked, that player shall leave the game until the next opportunity to substitute. The official shall enforce this rule at the next live ball after observing the violation.*

INTERPRETATION

Play: An official tells A1 to tuck in his or her game jersey and then issues a warning to the coach of Team A. Later in the game, A2 is fouled. Before giving A2 disposal of the ball for the free throw, the official notices that A2's game jersey is untucked. *Ruling:* A2 shall be permitted to attempt the free throw(s). When the free throw(s) are successful, he or she shall be instructed to leave the game. When the free throw(s) are not successful and he or she does not rectify the game-jersey violation before the next dead ball, A2 shall be instructed to leave the game.

Art. 3. Game jerseys shall be of the same single solid color.

Art. 4. The color, style and design of all teammates' game jerseys and game pants shall be alike.

Art. 5. Decorations permitted on game jerseys are:

a. Side inserts, including trim, no more than 4 inches wide of any color/design, centered vertically below the armpit and

b. Piping/trim not to exceed 1 inch around the neck and arm opening.

c. A logo or mascot at the center or apex of the neck-line of the game jersey.

Art. 6. Decorations such as mascots and stars are permissible only on the game jersey within the 4-inch side insert or anywhere on the game pants.

Art. 7. A commemorative/memorial patch or ribbon is permitted within the 4-inch side insert of the game jersey, anywhere on the game pants, anywhere on warm-up suits or on the shoulder strap of the game jersey. When the commemorative/memorial patch or ribbon is on the shoulder strap of the game jersey, it shall be sewn on or attached with Velcro.

Art. 8. Manufacturers' or distributors' labels or trademarks are not permitted on the game jersey.

Art. 9. An undershirt is considered to be part of the game jersey and must be a color similar to that of the game jersey. In addition, the sleeves and neckline of undershirts shall be unaltered (e.g., no cut-off sleeves or cut necklines) and both sleeves must be of the same length. No logos, decorations, trim, commemorative patches, lettering or numbering may be used on an undershirt. An illegal undershirt shall not be worn.

INTERPRETATION

Play: May a player remain in the game after being assessed an indirect technical foul for wearing an illegal undershirt or undergarment?

Ruling: Similar to the rule regarding jewelry, illegal undershirts or undergarments shall not be worn. The player shall remove the illegal apparel in order to play.

Art. 10. Tights that extend below the game pants must be similar in color to that of the game pants.

Art. 11. No more than two identifying names or abbreviations of the names may be placed on either, or on both, the front and back of the game jersey. The name(s) and/or abbreviation(s):

a. Shall identify the school, the school nickname or mascot, or the player's name.

b. Shall be placed vertically and/or horizontally. When placed horizontally, the lettering may be arched, but the first and last letters shall be in the same horizontal plane.

c. May be placed no closer than 1 inch from the top or bottom of the uniform number;

d. May have any form of decorative emphasis (e.g., paw, halo, crown, star) located above the name or abbreviation when the name or abbreviation is placed above the game jersey number; or

e. May have a tail or an underscore located below them when the name or abbreviation is placed below the game-jersey number.

f. Shall be placed such that the number(s) is clearly visible.

Art. 12. Each team member's game jersey shall be numbered on the front and back with plain Arabic numerals.

a. The following numbers are legal: 0, 1, 2, 3, 4, 5, 00, 10, 11, 12, 13, 14, 15, 20, 21, 22, 23, 24, 25, 30, 31, 32, 33, 34, 35, 40, 41, 42, 43, 44, 45, 50, 51, 52, 53, 54, 55. Team rosters can include 0 or 00 but not both. The numbers on the front and back of the game jersey shall be of the same color and style.

b. The number shall be at least 6 inches high on the back and at least 4 inches high on the front and not less than ¾ inch in width.

c. Numbers shall be centered on the front and back of game jerseys.

d. No more than three colors may be used on uniforms. The style used for the uniform number shall allow for the uniform number to be clearly visible and shall conform to one of the following:

1. A solid contrasting color with no more than two solid ¼-inch borders. A solid contrasting "shadow" trim, not to exceed ½ inch in width, may be used on part of the uniform number. When the game-jersey color is used as a border, it shall be counted as one of the allowed colors.

2. The game-jersey color itself shall be counted as one of the allowable colors when bordered with not more than two ¼-inch solid border(s) contrasting with the game-jersey color.

Art. 13. Members of the same squad shall not wear identical numbers.

a. When such an infraction occurs, the second-listed squad member in the official scorebook (and any following member) wearing an identical number shall be charged with an indirect technical foul. The penalty shall be imposed when the infraction is discovered.

b. When there is duplication, only one squad member shall be permitted to wear a given uniform number. All others must change to a uniform number not already in use before they may participate.

Art. 14. Opposing team uniforms shall be of contrasting colors. The home team should wear light game jerseys and the away team should wear dark game jerseys.

INTERPRETATION

Play: Contesting teams have uniforms of the same color.

Ruling: When possible, each team should have two sets of uniforms, one of light color and the other of dark color. The light color should be for home games. The team that violates this rule shall change. When there is doubt, the officials shall require the home team to change; on a neutral floor, the officials shall decide which team shall change.

Section 6. **Uniforms—Logos, Labels, Trademarks**

Game pants (but not game jerseys or T-shirts) and all other items of apparel (e.g., warm-ups, socks, headbands, wristbands and towels) may:

Art. 1. Bear only a single manufacturer's or distributor's normal logo, label or trademark.

a. The logo, label or trademark shall not exceed 2¼ square inches, including any additional material (e.g., patch) surrounding the normal trademark or logo.

b. The logo, label or trademark should be contained within a four-sided geometrical figure (i.e., rectangle, square, parallelogram).

Section 7. **Players' Equipment**

Art. 1. The referee shall not permit any player to wear equipment that in his or her judgment is dangerous to other players.

Art. 2. Elbow, hand, finger, wrist or forearm guards, casts or braces made of fiberglass, plaster, metal or any other non-pliable substance, shall be prohibited.

Art. 3. Pliable (flexible or easily bent) material, covered on all exterior sides and edges with no less than 1/2-inch thickness of a slow-rebounding foam, may be used to immobilize and/or protect an injury.

Art. 4. The prohibition of the use of hard-substance material does not apply to the upper arm, shoulder, thigh or lower leg when the material is padded so as not to create a hazard for other players.

Art. 5. Equipment that could cut or cause an injury to another player shall be prohibited, without respect to whether the equipment is hard. Excessively long finger-nails shall be prohibited.

Art. 6. Head decorations, head wear and jewelry are illegal. Headbands no wider than 2 inches made of nonabrasive, unadorned (except for the manufacturer's logo, which shall meet the size restrictions of Rule 3-6), single-color cloth, elastic, fiber, soft leather, pliable plastic or rubber shall be legal.

INTERPRETATIONS

Play 1: Substitute A6 attempts to enter the playing court wearing jewelry, an illegal headpiece or hat. ***Ruling:*** Substitute A6 shall not be permitted to enter before removing the jewelry, illegal headpiece or hat. A6 cannot "buy" his or her way into the game and the right to wear the illegal jewelry, illegal headpiece or hat by being charged with an indirect technical foul.

Play 2: Player A5 is found to be wearing jewelry. ***Ruling:*** The game shall be stopped. A5 shall be required to remove the jewelry immediately or be required to leave the game and not return until after removing the jewelry. A5 cannot "buy" the right to wear the jewelry by being charged with an indirect technical foul.

Art. 7. Any equipment that is unnatural and designed to increase a player's height or reach, or to gain an unfair advantage, shall be prohibited.

Art. 8. Equipment used shall be appropriate for basketball. Basketball knee braces may be worn if they are covered properly. A protector for a broken nose, even though made of hard material, shall be permissible when it does not endanger other players. Eyeglass protectors are appropriate equipment when they meet the qualifications outlined in this Rule.

Rule 4

Definitions

Rule 4

Definitions

Section 1. **Airborne Shooter**

Art. 1. An airborne shooter is a player who has released the ball on a try for goal until one foot has returned to the floor.

Art. 2. An airborne shooter is in the act of shooting.

INTERPRETATION

Play: A1 is in the air on a jump shot in the lane. A1 releases the ball on a try and is fouled by B1, who has jumped in an unsuccessful attempt to block the shot. A1's try is: (a) successful; or (b) unsuccessful.

Ruling: A1 shall be an airborne shooter when the ball is released until he or she returns with one foot touching the floor. An airborne shooter shall be in the act of shooting. B1 has fouled A1 in the act of shooting. A1 shall be awarded one free throw in (a), and two in (b).

Section 2. **Alternating-Possession Procedure**

Art. 1. The alternating-possession procedure is a method of putting the ball in play with a throw-in rather than a jump ball.

Art. 2. The alternating-possession procedure starts when an official places the ball at the disposal of a player for a throw-in and ends when the throw-in is completed or when the throw-in team commits a violation.

Art. 3. The team awarded the ball for the alternating-possession throw-in shall be indicated by the alternating-possession arrow.

Section 3. **Basket**

Art. 1. Each basket consists of the 18-inch ring, its flange and braces, and appended net through which players attempt to throw or tap the ball.

Art. 2. A team's own basket is the one into which its players try to throw or tap the ball. Each team shall warm up and shoot during the first half at the basket farthest from its bench.

Art. 3. The teams shall change baskets for the second half.

Art. 4. When the official(s) permits a team to go in the wrong direction, and when the error is discovered (a) all points scored, (b) fouls committed and (c) time consumed shall count as though each team had gone in the proper direction. Play shall be resumed with each team going in the proper direction.

Section 4. **Basket Interference**

Art. 1. Basket interference occurs when a player:

a. Touches the ball or any part of the basket while the ball is on or within the basket,

b. Touches the ball while any part of it is within the cylinder that has the ring as its lower base, or

c. Reaches through the basket from below and touches the ball before it enters the cylinder.

INTERPRETATIONS

Play 1: The ball is touching the side of the ring of Team A. B1 jumps and contacts the net. The ball is not touching the top of the ring.

Ruling: No violation. The ball shall remain live.

Play 2: While the ball is touching the top of the ring on a field-goal attempt, a player grasps the ring.

Ruling: Double infraction. Both basket interference and an indirect technical foul shall be called. The moment the hand touched the ring, it was basket interference. When the player grasped the ring, an indirect technical foul occurred. (See Rule 10-3.12.)

Play 3: The ball enters the basket during a field-goal try by A1. Before the ball is in flight for the try, A1 is fouled. A2 touches the ring while the ball is in the basket.

Ruling: Basket interference on A2. The goal shall be canceled. A1 shall be awarded two free throws because of the foul.

Play 4: A1 rebounds the ball while part of the ball is in the cylinder and, in the same continuous motion, dunks.

Ruling: Basket interference. The ball shall be ruled dead when A1 contacts the ball in the cylinder, and the dunking of the dead ball shall be ignored. The basket shall be disallowed.

Art. 2. Basket interference also occurs when a movable basket ring is pulled down by a player so that it contacts the ball before the ring returns to its original position.

Section 5.   Batting the Ball
Art. 1. Batting the ball is intentionally striking the ball or intentionally changing its direction with the hand or arm.

Section 6.   Bench Personnel
Art. 1. Bench personnel includes anyone in the team bench area and substitutes.

Section 7.   Blocking
Art. 1. Blocking is illegal personal contact that impedes the progress of an opponent.

Section 8.   Charging

Art. 1. Charging is illegal personal contact by pushing or moving into an opponent's torso.

INTERPRETATIONS

Play 1: (**Men**) B1 is standing behind the backboard before A1 jumps for a layup. The forward momentum of A1 causes contact with B1.

Ruling: B1 is entitled to the position provided that there was no movement into such position by B1 after A1 leaped from the floor. When the ball goes through the basket before the contact occurs, the contact shall be ignored unless B1 has been placed at a disadvantage by being unable to rebound when the shot is missed or unable to put the ball in play without delay, when the try was successful. When the contact occurs before the ball becomes dead, a charging foul has been committed by A1. When B1 moves into the path of A1 after A1 has left the floor, the foul shall be on B1. It shall be an intentional foul when a player moves into the path of an airborne opponent with the intent to undercut and contact results. When the moving player moves under the airborne opponent and there is danger of severe injury as a result of the contact, it shall be a flagrant personal foul on the moving player.

Play 2: (**Women**) B1 is standing directly under the basket before A1 jumps for a layup. The forward momentum of airborne shooter A1 causes A1 to run into B1.

Ruling: B1 is not in a legal guarding position. Blocking foul on B1.

Section 9.   Bonus Free Throws

Art. 1. One type of a bonus free throw is a second free throw that is awarded for each common foul (except a player-control foul) committed by a player of a team, beginning with that team's seventh foul in a half, which is a combination of personal fouls, direct technical fouls, intentional technical fouls and flagrant technical fouls, provided that the first free throw for the foul is successful.

Art. 2. Beginning with the 10th team foul in a half, which is a combination of personal fouls, direct technical fouls, intentional technical fouls and flagrant technical fouls, two free throws shall be awarded for each common foul (except a player-control foul).

INTERPRETATION

Play: The bonus is in effect; and, while the ball is in flight during a try for a field goal, A1 charges into B1, which is Team A's seventh foul in the half. After this, there is a basket-interference violation by: (a) B2, or (b) A2.

Ruling: (a) Both the personal foul by A1 and the violation by B2 shall be penalized, but in the reverse order of occurrence. First, two points shall be awarded to Team A because of the violation by B2; B1 shall be awarded a one-and-one, and the ball shall remain live when the last throw is not successful and it touches the ring or flange. When A1's foul is Team A's 10th foul or higher in a half, including any combination of those described in Rule 4-9.2, award two shots and the ball remains in play. Beginning with the 10th foul in a half, including any combination of those described in Rule 4-9.2, two shots shall be awarded for each common foul (except player-control). In (b), there are no rule complications. The violation caused the ball to become dead. Ordinarily, the ball would go to Team B at a designated spot. However, this penalty shall be ignored because of the penalty enforcement for the foul by A1. Had the bonus rule not been in effect, the ball would be awarded to Team B at a designated spot. (See Rule 9-16.3.)

Art. 3. A player-control foul shall count as a team foul for reaching the bonus.

Art. 4. All direct technical fouls charged to bench personnel shall count toward the team-foul total and bonus.

Section 10. Boundary Lines

Art. 1. Boundary lines of the playing court shall consist of end lines and sidelines. The inside edges of these lines define the inbounds and out-of-bounds areas.

Section 11. Closely Guarded

Art. 1. (Men) A player in control in the front court only while holding or dribbling the ball is closely guarded when his opponent is in a guarding stance at a distance not exceeding 6 feet.

Art. 2. (Women) A player in control anywhere on the playing court while holding (not dribbling) the ball is closely guarded when her opponent is in a guarding stance at a distance not exceeding 6 feet.

Art. 3. After the start of a five-second closely guarded count, in order for a closely guarded violation to occur, there shall be continuous guarding by the same opponent.

Art. 4. When a player is positioned between the player in control of the ball and his or her opponent, who is within 6 feet, a closely guarded situation does not exist.

Section 12. Continuous Motion

Art. 1. Continuous motion applies to a try for field goal or free throw, but shall have no significance unless there is a foul by the defense during the interval that begins when the habitual throwing movement starts a try or with the touching on a tap and ends when the ball is clearly in flight.

Section 13. In Control—Player, Team

Art. 1. A player shall be in control when holding a live ball or dribbling it while inbounds.

Art. 2. A team shall be in control when a player of the team is in control and also while a live ball is being passed between teammates.

Art. 3. Team control shall continue until the ball is in flight during a try for goal, an opponent secures control or the ball becomes dead.

Art. 4. There shall be no team control during:

a. A jump ball;
b. A throw-in;
c. The tapping of a rebound (unless it is a try for goal);
d. A try for goal after the ball is in flight;
e. The period that follows any of these acts (a-d) while the ball is being batted (from the vicinity of other players) in an attempt to secure control;
f. A dead ball.

Art. 5. Team control is re-established in Article 4 of this Rule when a player secures control.

Art. 6. "Control" for purposes of establishing the alternating-possession procedure occurs when:

a. A player is in control;
b. The ball is handed/bounced to or placed at the disposal of the free-thrower after a common foul; or
c. The ball is handed/bounced to or placed at the disposal of the thrower-in.

Section 14. Cylinder

Art 1. The cylinder is the imaginary geometric figure that has the ring as its base and is formed by the upward extension of that ring.

Section 15. Designated Spot

Art. 1. A designated spot is the location at which a thrower-in is presented disposal of the ball out of bounds nearest to where a rules infraction or held ball occurred, or at the out-of-bounds location at the division line or free-throw line extended to the sideline.

Art. 2. A designated spot shall be 3 feet wide with no depth limitation.

Art. 3. Leaving the designated spot during a designated-spot throw-in shall be a violation.

Section 16. Disposal of Ball

Art. 1. The ball is at the disposal of a player when it is:
a. Handed to the thrower-in or free-thrower,
b. Caught by the thrower-in or the free-thrower after it is bounced to him or her,
c. Placed at a spot on the floor or
d. Available to a player after a goal.

Section 17. Disqualified Player

Art. 1. A disqualified player is one who is barred from further participation in a game because of:
a. Committing a fifth foul, including personal fouls, direct technical fouls and intentional technical fouls;
b. Committing a flagrant foul;
c. Participating after changing his or her uniform number without reporting it to the scorers and an official;
d. Ejection; or
e. Participating after having been disqualified.

Art. 2. A team member who leaves the bench area during a fight shall be disqualified.

Art. 3. The officials shall notify the coach and player of any disqualification.

Art. 4. When the coach is notified by an official that a player is disqualified, that player becomes bench personnel.

INTERPRETATION

Play: A5 is fouled during an unsuccessful try for goal. As A5 goes to the free-throw line, A5 is assessed an unsporting technical foul, which is A5's fifth and disqualifying foul. The scorer (a) informs the official that A5 has been disqualified or (b) does not inform the scorer that A5 has been disqualified and A5 attempts the free throws.

Ruling: In (a), any Team B member shall attempt the free throws. In (b), since A5 and A5's coach were not notified of the disqualification, the results of the free throws stand.

Art. 5. A disqualified player shall be replaced within a 30-second time limit. A signal shall be sounded both 15 seconds before the expiration of this time limit and at the end of the time limit, with the latter signal indicating that play shall resume.

Section 18. **Dribble**

Art. 1. A dribble is ball movement caused by a player in control who bats, pushes or taps the ball to the playing court once or several times.

INTERPRETATION

Play 1: In the front court of Team A (the back court of Team B), A1 passes the ball to A2. B1, in an attempt to secure the ball, bats it down the

playing court toward B's basket. The ball bounces
several times before B1 can recover it in B's front
court. B1 dribbles to B's basket and scores.
Ruling: Legal. The bat of the ball by B1 shall not
be considered part of the dribble. B1 does not have
control of the ball until securing it after batting it.

Art. 2. The dribble may be started by pushing, throwing, tapping or batting the ball to the playing court.
Art. 3. During a dribble, the ball may be batted into the
air, provided that it is permitted to strike the playing
court one or more times before the ball is touched
again with either hand.
Art. 4. The dribble ends when:
a. The dribbler catches or carries/palms the ball by
   allowing it to come to rest in one or both hands.
b. The dribbler touches the ball with both hands
   simultaneously.
c. An opponent bats the ball.
d. The ball becomes dead.

INTERPRETATIONS

Play 1: A1, while advancing the ball by dribbling,
manages to keep a hand in contact with the ball
until it reaches its maximum height. A1 maintains
such control as the ball descends, pushing it to the
playing court at the last moment; however, after six
or seven bounces, A1's hands are in contact with
the ball and the palm of the hand on this particular
dribble is skyward.
Ruling: Violation. The ball has come to rest on the
hand while the palm and the fingers are facing
upward, so the dribble has ended. When the player
continues to move or stand still and dribble, the
player has committed a violation by dribbling a second time. (See Rule 9-6.)

Play 2: Is a player dribbling while touching the ball during a jump, when a pass rebounds from the player's hand, when the player fumbles or when the player tips a rebound or pass away from other players who are attempting to get it?

Ruling: No. The player is not in control under these conditions and therefore is not dribbling.

Play 3: A1 dribbles and comes to a stop, after which A1 throws the ball: (a) against the opponent's backboard and catches the rebound; or (b) against the official, immediately recovering the ball and dribbling again.

Ruling: A1 has committed a violation in both (a) and (b). Throwing the ball against an opponent's backboard or an official constitutes another dribble, provided that A1 is first to touch the ball after it strikes the official or the backboard.

Play 4: A1 is dribbling the ball when: (a) A1 bats the ball over the head of an opponent, runs around the opponent, bats the ball to the playing court and continues to dribble or (b) A1 fumbles the ball in an attempt to complete his or her dribble and causes the ball to roll out of reach so that A1 must run to recover it.

Ruling: Violation in (a) because the ball is touched twice during a dribble, before the ball touches the playing court. In (b), it is illegal to continue to dribble but A1 may recover the ball.

Art. 5. An interrupted dribble occurs when the ball is loose after deflecting off the dribbler or after it momentarily gets away from the dribbler.

Art. 6. During an interrupted dribble, there shall be no player control and the following cannot occur:

a. Three-second lane violation.

---

b. Player-control foul.
c. Acknowledgement of a timeout request.
d. (**Men**) Five-second closely guarded dribbling violation.

INTERPRETATION

Play: A1 is dribbling the ball in the front court when the ball momentarily gets away from him or her. While the dribble is interrupted: (a) A1 pushes B2 while trying to retrieve the ball; (b) A2 is in the lane for four seconds; and (c) A1 calls a timeout. *Ruling:* (a) Common foul called on A1; (b) lane violations are not in effect during an interrupted dribble; and (c) a timeout shall not be acknowledged during an interrupted dribble.

Section 19. Dunk

Art. 1. A dunk occurs when any player gains control of a ball that is neither in the cylinder nor on the ring and then attempts to drive, force or stuff the ball through the basket.

Section 20. Ejection

Art. 1. Ejection is the act of dismissing an individual from participation in a game because of a specific infraction of the rules.

a. In addition to being disqualified, an individual who is ejected shall leave the playing court and floor area and report to his or her team's locker room until the game is over.

Section 21. Entering Player

Art. 1. An entering player is a substitute who has been beckoned onto the playing court by an official.

Section 22.   Extra Period

Art. 1. An extra period is the extension of playing time allocated to break a tie score.

Art. 2. The length of each extra period shall be five minutes.

Section 23.   Fighting

Art. 1. Fighting is an attempt to strike an opponent with the arms, hands, legs or feet, or a combative action by one or more players, a coach or other team personnel.

Art. 2. For any flagrant foul that is deemed to be a fight, the fighting penalty shall be invoked.

Art. 3. Combative action includes but is not exclusive to:

a. A player, coach or other team personnel attempting to punch or kick an opponent; whether there is contact with an opponent is irrelevant.

b. A player, coach or other team personnel who, in the opinion of a game official, instigates a fight by perpetrating an unsporting act toward an opponent that causes the opponent to retaliate by fighting.

Section 24.   Followers

Art. 1. Followers are fans, bands, cheerleaders and mascots.

Section 25.   Forfeit/No Contest

Art. 1. A forfeit is the termination of the game by the referee.

Art. 2. A "no contest" is when a team does not appear at the game site due to inclement weather, an accident, vehicle breakdown, illness or catastrophic cause. An institution shall not, for statistical purposes, declare a forfeit for non-fulfillment of a contract, but rather shall

---

declare a "no contest." When officials are not present or available to officiate, there cannot be a sanctioned game/contest.

Section 26. Foul

A foul is an infraction of the rules that is charged to a squad member or a coach and is penalized in various ways. Following are the types of fouls:

Art. 1. Personal foul. A personal foul shall be a foul committed by a player that involves illegal contact with an opponent while the ball is live.

Art. 2. Common foul. A common foul shall be a personal foul that is neither flagrant nor intentional, nor committed against a player trying for a field goal, nor part of a double or multiple foul.

Art. 3. Indirect and Direct Technical foul. A technical foul that is direct or indirect shall be a foul by any player, squad member, coach or bench personnel that does not involve contact with an opponent or causes contact with an opponent while the ball is dead. Examples of indirect and direct technical fouls shall include:

a. Unsporting conduct (direct),
b. Requesting an excessive timeout (indirect) and
c. Hanging on the ring, except when doing so to prevent an injury (indirect).

Art. 4. Flagrant personal foul, live ball. A flagrant personal foul shall be a personal foul that involves severe or excessive contact with an opponent while the ball is live.

Art. 5. Flagrant technical foul, dead ball. A flagrant foul shall be a technical foul when it involves either unsporting conduct that is extreme in nature, or severe, excessive contact against an opponent while the ball is dead.

a. An exception is a foul by an airborne shooter.

Art. 6. Intentional personal foul. An intentional foul shall be a personal foul that, on the basis of an official's observation of the act, is not a legitimate attempt to directly play the ball or a player. Determination of whether a personal foul is intentional shall not be based on the severity of the act. Examples include, but are not limited to:

a. Fouling a player who is away from the ball and not directly involved with the play.
b. Contact with a player making a throw-in.
c. Holding or pushing an opponent in order to stop the game clock.
d. Pushing a player from behind to prevent a score.
e. Causing excessive contact with an opponent while playing the ball.

INTERPRETATION

Play: After a field goal by B1, Team A leads Team B, 61-60. A1 has the ball for a throw-in with four seconds remaining in the game. A1 holds the ball and B2 crosses the boundary line to hold A1.
Ruling: An intentional personal foul shall be charged to B2. The time remaining to play is not a factor. This circumstance shall not permit a warning.

Art. 7. Intentional technical foul. An intentional technical foul involves intentionally contacting an opponent in a non-flagrant manner when the ball is dead.
Art. 8. Player-control foul. A player-control foul is a common foul committed:
a. (**Men**) By a player when he is in control of the ball.
b. (**Women**) By a player when she is in control of the ball or by an airborne shooter.

INTERPRETATIONS

Play 1: (**Women**) A1 ends the dribble, passes the ball to A2 and charges into B2: (a) while the ball is in the air; or (b) after A2 has control.

Ruling: The foul on A1 in both (a) and (b) is not a player-control foul since A1 was not holding or dribbling the ball and was not an airborne shooter in either situation. In (a), when the official is in doubt as to whether the charging occurred before or after the ball was released on the pass, the charge should not be ruled a player-control foul.

Play 2: (**Women**) Is it possible for airborne shooter A1 to commit a foul that would not be a player-control foul?

Ruling: Yes. The airborne shooter could be charged with an intentional, personal or flagrant personal foul or with a technical foul. None of these fouls can be player control. When an airborne shooter commits a foul that is not a player-control foul, the infraction shall be penalized as dictated by the type of foul.

Play 3: (**Women**) Airborne A1 is fouled by B1 during a try for a field goal. A1 releases the ball then illegally contacts B2 in returning to the floor after the shot. The ball goes through the basket.

Ruling: This shall be a false double foul. The foul by B1 did not cause the ball to become dead since A1 had started the trying motion. However, airborne shooter A1's foul shall be a player-control foul that causes the ball to become dead immediately. No goal can be scored even when the ball goes through the basket before the foul. Since the try is unsuccessful, A1 shall be awarded two free throws for the foul by B1. No players shall be

allowed in lane spaces since Team B shall be
awarded the ball after the last free throw. When the
last free throw is successful, the throw-in shall be
from anywhere along the end line. When the last
free throw is unsuccessful, the throw-in shall be
from a designated spot.

Art. 9. Double personal foul. A double personal foul
occurs when two opponents commit personal fouls
against each other at approximately the same time.

Art. 10. Double technical foul. A double technical foul
occurs when opponents commit technical fouls against
each other at approximately the same time.

Art. 11. False double foul. A false double foul occurs
when there are fouls by both teams, the second of
which occurs before the game clock is started after it is
stopped for the first but such that at least one of the
attributes of a double foul is absent.

INTERPRETATIONS

Play 1: B1 commits a common foul on A1 before
the bonus is in effect for either team. The ball shall
be awarded to Team A at the designated spot. A2
fouls B2 during the throw-in before the game clock
is started. Team B is in the bonus.

Ruling: The foul by A2 shall result in a false double
foul. B2 shall be awarded a one-and-one. When
both free throws are successful, the ball shall be
awarded to Team A for a throw-in from any point
behind the end line. When either free throw is
missed, the ball shall be in play when it touches the
ring. (See Rule 8-6.1.)

Play 2: A1 is entitled to a one-and-one free throw.
Before the ball is handed to A1, Team A's coach is
assessed a direct technical foul.

> ***Ruling:*** The direct technical foul creates a false double foul. Team B shall be awarded two free throws because of the direct technical foul on coach A. After Team B shoots the free throws for the technical fouls, A1 shall attempt the one-and-one since that was the point of interruption.

Art. 12. Multiple foul. A multiple foul occurs when two or more teammates commit personal fouls against the same opponent at approximately the same time.

Art. 13. False multiple foul. A false multiple foul occurs when there are two or more fouls by the same team such that the last foul is committed before the game clock is started after it is stopped for the first, and such that at least one of the attributes of a multiple foul is absent.

Art. 14. Simultaneous technical foul. A simultaneous technical foul can be direct or indirect and occurs when there is a technical foul committed by each team, at approximately the same time, not by opponents against each other.

Art. 15. Simultaneous personal foul. A simultaneous personal foul by opponents occurs when a personal foul is committed by each team at approximately the same time but not by opponents against each other.

Section 27. Free Throw

Art. 1. A free throw is the privilege given a player to score one point by an unhindered try for goal from within the free-throw semicircle and behind the free-throw line.

Art. 2. A free throw starts when the ball is placed at the disposal of the free-thrower.

Art. 3. A free throw ends when:

a. The try is successful;

b. It is certain the try will not be successful;

c. The try touches the floor or any player; or

d. The ball becomes dead.

Section 28. Front Court/Back Court

Art. 1. A team's front court shall consist of that part of the playing court between its end line and the nearer edge of the division line, including its basket and the inbounds part of its backboard.

Art. 2. A team's back court consists of the rest of the playing court, including its opponent's basket and inbounds part of the backboard and the division line, excluding the mathematical edge nearest the team's basket.

Art. 3. A live ball is in the front court or back court of the team in control as follows:

a. A ball that is in contact with a player or with the playing court shall be in the back court when either the ball or the player (either player when the ball is touching more than one) is touching the back court. It shall be in the front court when neither the ball nor the player is touching the back court.

b. A ball that is not in contact with a player or the playing court retains the same status as when it was last in contact with a player or the playing court.

INTERPRETATION

Play: As Team A advances the ball from its back court toward its front court, A1 passes the ball to A2. A2 catches the ball while both feet are on the playing court with one foot on either side of the division line. In this situation, either foot may be the pivot foot. (a) A2 lifts the foot that is in the back court and then puts it back on the floor in the back court; or (b) A2 lifts the foot that is in the front court, pivots and puts it on the floor in the back court.

Ruling: In (a), back-court violation. When A2, while holding the ball, lifts the foot that was in the back court, the ball is in the front court. When A2's foot touches in the back court, it shall be a violation. In (b), when A2 lifts the foot that is in the front court and places it down in the back court, the location of the ball has not changed. The ball is still in the back court and no violation has occurred. (See Rule 4-28.2.)

c. During a dribble from back court to front court, the ball shall be in the front court when both feet of the dribbler and the ball touch the playing court entirely in the front court.

Section 29. Fumble

Art. 1. A fumble shall be the accidental loss of player control when the ball unintentionally drops or slips from a player's grasp.

INTERPRETATION

Play: A1, on a throw-in from a designated spot, fumbles. A1 leaves the designated spot to retrieve the fumble. Is this a violation?

Ruling: Provided that A1 retrieves the ball and returns to the designated spot and releases the throw-in within the five-second requirement, it shall not be a violation.

Section 30. Game Clock

Art. 1. The game clock shall be the official, visible time-piece on which the time remaining in a period shall be displayed.

Section 31.   Goal

Art. 1. A goal shall be made when a live ball enters the basket from above and remains in or passes through, except on a throw-in.

Art. 2. Whether the game clock is running or stopped shall have no influence on the counting of a goal.

Section 32.   Goaltending

Art. 1. Goaltending shall have occured when a player touches the ball during a field-goal try and each of the following conditions is met:

a.   The ball is in its downward flight,

b.   The entire ball is above the level of the ring and has the possibility, while in flight, of entering the basket and is not touching the cylinder.

Art. 2. It is goaltending to touch the ball outside the cylinder during a free throw, regardless of whether the free throw is on its upward or downward flight.

Section 33   Guarding

Art. 1. Guarding shall be the act of legally placing the body in the path of an offensive opponent.

Art. 2. There is no minimum distance required between the guard and opponent, but the maximum shall be 6 feet when closely guarded. The 6-foot distance shall apply only when a player is holding the ball (for **men**, this distance also applies while dribbling).

Art. 3. Every player shall be entitled to a spot on the playing court, provided that such player gets there first without illegally contacting an opponent.

Art. 4. The guard may shift to maintain guarding position in the path of the dribbler, provided that the guard does not charge into the dribbler nor otherwise cause contact as in Rule 10-19.2 and 10-19.3.

Art. 5. The responsibility of the dribbler for contact shall not be shifted merely because the guard turns or

ducks to absorb shock when contact caused by the
dribbler is imminent.

Art. 6. To establish an initial legal guarding position on
the player with the ball:

a. The guard shall have both feet touching the playing
   court. When the guard jumps into position
   initially, both feet must return to the playing court
   after the jump, for the guard to attain a guarding
   position.
b. The guard's torso shall face the opponent.
c. No time and distance shall be required.
d. When the opponent with the ball is airborne, the
   guard shall have attained legal position before the
   opponent left the playing court.

INTERPRETATION

> *Play:* B1 takes a spot on the playing court before
> A1 jumps to catch a pass. (a) A1 returns to the play-
> ing court and lands on B1, or (b) B1 moves to a
> new spot while A1 is airborne. A1 comes to the
> floor on one foot and then charges into B1.
> *Ruling:* In both (a) and (b), the foul shall be on A1.

Art. 7. To establish legal guarding position on a player
without the ball:

a. Time and distance shall be required to attain an initial legal position.
b. The guard shall give the opponent the time and distance to avoid contact.

INTERPRETATION

> *Play:* A1 runs toward Team A's goal and looks back
> to receive a fast-break outlet pass. B1 takes a
> position in the path of A1 while A1 is 10 feet away
> from B1. (a) A1 runs into B1 before receiving the

ball; or (b) A1 receives the ball and, before taking a step, contacts B1.

Ruling: In both (a) and (b), A1 shall be held responsible for contact. B1 took a position in the path of A1 that was far enough away from A1 to avoid contact.

c. The distance given by the opponent of the player without the ball need not be more than two strides.

d. When the opponent is airborne, the guard shall have attained legal position before the opponent left the playing court.

Section 34. Hands and Arms, Use of

Art. 1. The arms may be extended vertically above one's shoulder and need not be lowered to avoid contact with an opponent when the action of the opponent causes contact.

a. This legal use of the arms and hands usually occurs when guarding:
   1. The thrower-in
   2. The player with the ball in pressing tactics or
   3. A player with the ball who is maneuvering to try for goal by pivoting, jumping or hooking either a pass or try for goal.

Art. 2. It shall be legal for a defender to accidentally hit the hand of a ball-handler when reaching to block or slap the ball when there is player control with that player's hand in contact with the ball and when that player is a:

a. Dribbler

b. Player attempting a try for field goal, or

c. Player holding the ball.

Art. 3. A player shall be permitted to hold his or her hands and arms in front of his or her face or body for protection in a recoil action rather than a pushing action . . .

a. To absorb force from imminent contact by an opponent or

b. When that player, who has set a blind screen, is about to be run into by the player being screened.

Art. 4. A player shall not use the arms, hands, hips or shoulders . . .

a. To force his or her way through a screen or

b. To hold the screener and then push the screener aside in order to maintain a guarding position relative to his or her opponent.

Art. 5. It shall be illegal to extend one's arms fully or partially, other than vertically, so that the freedom of movement of an opponent is hindered when contact with the extended arms occurs.

Art. 6. It shall be illegal to extend one's elbow(s) when one's . . .

a. Hands are on one's hips,

b. Hands are held near one's chest or

c. Arms are held approximately horizontal to the playing court.

Note: *These illegal positions are most commonly used when rebounding, screening or in the various aspects of post play.*

Art. 7. The following shall be considered excessive swinging:

a. When arm(s) and elbow(s) are swung about while using the shoulders as pivots, and the speed of the extended arm(s) and elbow(s) exceeds that of the rest of the body as it rotates on the hips or on the pivot foot; or

b. When the speed and vigor with which the arm(s) and elbow(s) are swung is such that injury could result if another player were contacted.

Section 35.   Held Ball

Art. 1. A held ball occurs when an opponent places his or her hand(s):

a. So firmly on the ball that control cannot be obtained without undue roughness.

b. On the ball to prevent an airborne player from throwing the ball or attempting a try.

INTERPRETATIONS

Play 1: A1 jumps for a try for field goal. B1 jumps to defend against the try and (a) touches the ball before it leaves A1's hand and A1 returns to the floor with the ball and the ball never loses contact with A1's hand(s) or (b) the ball loses contact with A1's hand(s), A1 retrieves the ball while in the air and returns to the floor in possession of the ball and begins to dribble or (c) after the ball touches the floor, A1 recovers the ball and begins to dribble.
Ruling: In (a), the official shall call a held ball. In (b) and (c), the play shall be legal. A1 has gained a new possession in both instances.

Play 2: A1 jumps to throw the ball. B1 prevents the throw by placing one or both hands on the ball and: (a) A1, or (b) A1 and B1 both return to the playing court holding the ball.
Ruling: Held ball. However, when A1 voluntarily drops the ball before returning to the playing court and then touches the ball before it is touched by another player, A1 has committed a violation for the illegal start of a dribble.

Play 3: Team A has been awarded a throw-in after a violation. A1, during the throw-in, breaks the boundary plane with the ball and extends the ball over the playing court. B1 causes a held ball. The possession arrow favors Team A.

> ***Ruling:*** A1's breaking the boundary plane and
> extending the ball over the playing court does not
> violate throw-in provisions. B1 legally grabbed a
> live ball and caused a held ball. The ball shall be
> awarded to Team A for an alternating-possession
> procedure.

Section 36. Holding

Art. 1. Holding is illegal personal contact with an opponent that interferes with the opponent's freedom of movement.

Section 37. Incidental Contact

Art. 1. Contact shall not constitute a foul. When 10 players move rapidly in a limited area, some contact is certain to occur. Incidental contact shall be contact with an opponent that is permitted and does not constitute a foul.

Art. 2. Contact that is incidental to an effort by an opponent to reach a loose ball, or contact that results when opponents are in equally favorable positions to perform normal defensive or offensive movement, should be permitted even though the contact may be severe or excessive.

Art. 3. Contact that does not hinder the opponent from participating in normal defensive or offensive movements shall be considered incidental.

Art. 4. A player who is screened within his or her visual field shall be expected to avoid contact with the screener by stopping or avoiding the screener.

Art. 5. A player who is screened outside his or her visual field may make inadvertent contact with the screener. Such contact shall be incidental, provided that the screener is not displaced when he or she has the ball.

Art. 6. When a player approaches an opponent from behind or a position from which the player has no reasonable chance to play the ball without making contact with the opponent, the responsibility for contact shall be that of the player in the unfavorable position.

Section 38. Intermission

Art. 1. Intermission is the time between the first and second periods and any extra period(s).

a. Cheerleaders/dance teams and mascots are allowed on the playing court and bands, musical instruments, or recorded music can play or be played during intermission(s).

Section 39. Jump Ball

Art. 1. A jump ball is a method of putting the ball into play at the beginning of the game or any extra period(s) by tossing it up between two opponents in the center circle.

Art. 2. A jump ball shall begin when the ball leaves the official's hand and shall end when it touches a non-jumper, the floor, basket or backboard.

Section 40. Jumpers

Art. 1. Jumpers are the two opposing players vying for the tip during a jump ball.

Section 41. Kicking the Ball

Art. 1. Kicking the ball is striking it intentionally with any part of the leg or the foot.

Art. 2. Accidentally striking the ball with the foot or leg shall not be a violation.

Section 42. Location of a Player

Art. 1. The location of a player (or non-player) is determined as being:

a. Where he or she is touching the floor, as far as being inbounds or out of bounds.

b. In the front court or back court.

c. Outside or inside the three-point line.

Art. 2. When a player is in the air from a leap (except during a throw-in) or when a defensive player intercepts a ball while in the air, the player's status with reference to these two situations shall be the same as at the time the player was last in contact with the floor or an extension of the floor, such as a bleacher.

Art. 3. When the ball touches an official who is on the playing court, play shall continue as if the ball touched the floor at the official's location.

INTERPRETATION

Play: An official is in the front court when he or she runs into a pass thrown by A1 from Team A's back court. After touching the official, the ball (a) goes out of bounds or (b) rebounds to the back court, where it is recovered by A3.

Ruling: Touching the official shall be the same as touching the floor where the official is standing. In (a), the ball shall be awarded to Team B for a throw-in. In (b), since A1 was the last player to touch the ball before it returns to the back court, A1 caused it to go there. Back-court violation. (See Rule 9-11.1.)

Section 43. **Multiple Free Throw**

Art. 1. A multiple free throw is a succession of free throws attempted by the same team.

Section 44. **Pass**

Art. 1. A pass is movement of the ball caused by a player who throws, bats or rolls the ball to another player.

Section 45. **Penalty**

Art. 1. A penalty for a foul is the charging of the offender with the foul and awarding one or more free throws, or awarding the ball to the opponent for a throw-in.

Art. 2. The penalty for a violation is the awarding of the ball to the opponent for a throw-in, one or more points or a substitute free throw.

Section 46. **Pivot**

Art. 1. A pivot takes place when a player who is holding the ball steps once or more than once in any direction with the same foot, while the other foot, called the pivot foot, is kept at its point of contact with the playing court.

Section 47. **Player**

Art. 1. A player is one of five or fewer members of a team's personnel who is legally on the playing court.

Section 48. **Playing Court**

Art. 1. The playing court is the area on the floor that lies within the geometrical lines formed by the inside edge of the boundary lines.

Section 49. **Point of Interruption**

Art. 1. Point of interruption is where the ball was located when the whistle sounded.

Section 50. **Post Player**

Art. 1. A post player is an offensive or defensive player with or without the ball with his or her back to the basket who is inside the free-throw lane or just outside the lane.

Section 51. Rebound

Art. 1. A rebound is an attempt by any player to secure possession of the ball after a try for goal. In a rebounding situation, there is no player or team control.

Art. 2. To attain or maintain legal rebounding position, a player shall not:

a. Displace, charge or push an opponent.
b. Extend either or both shoulders, hips, knees or extend either or both arms or elbows fully or partially in a position other than vertical so that the freedom of movement of an opponent is hindered when contact with any of these body parts occurs.
c. Bend his/her body in an abnormal position to hold or displace an opponent.
d. Violate the principle of verticality.

Art. 3. Every player shall be entitled to a spot on the playing court, provided that such player gets there first without illegally contacting an opponent.

Section 52. Resumption of Play

Art. 1. Resumption of play is the method of putting the ball in play by placing the ball at the disposal of the player. The resumption of play is in effect for the entire game except to start the second half.

INTERPRETATION

Play: After a timeout, Team A is entitled to the ball for a throw-in. The referee blows the whistle indicating that the timeout is over. When Team A is not at the designated spot ready to take the ball, the referee shall place the ball on the floor out of bounds at the disposal of Team A. The visible count begins and: (a) A1 picks up the ball and releases it for the throw-in within the allotted five seconds; (b) Team A does not pick up the ball within five seconds; (c) because Team A did not comply with throw-in provisions after a timeout, Team B is entitled to possession for a throw-in, but Team B does not get to the designated spot within five seconds after the referee places the ball on the floor at Team B's disposal.

Ruling: In (a), legal play. In (b), violation on Team A. The referee shall blow the whistle and begin a five-second count when the ball is handed to Team B for the throw-in or placed on the floor at Team B's disposal. In (c), violation on Team B. The referee shall assess a double indirect technical foul. Each team shall be penalized for delay of game. No free throws shall be shot by either team. Play shall resume at the point of interruption.

Section 53. Rule

Art. 1. A rule is one of the groups of laws that govern the game.

Art. 2. A game law (commonly called a rule) sometimes states or implies that the ball is dead or a foul or violation is involved. When it does not, it shall be assumed that the ball is live and no foul or violation has occurred to affect the given situation.

Art. 3. A single infraction shall not be complicated by a second infraction unless so stated or implied.

Section 54. Scorebook

Art. 1. The scorebook is the book or form in which the official scorer records the statistics of the game.

Section 55. Screen

Art. 1. A screen is legal action by a player who, without causing contact, delays or prevents an opponent from reaching a desired position.

Art. 2. In screening tactics, the screener shall not be required to face in any particular direction at any time.

Art. 3. The screener shall not lean into the path of an opponent or extend his or her hips into that path, even though his or her feet are stationary.

Art. 4. A player with the ball may be a screener and shall be subject to the principles of screening.

Art. 5. While most screening is by the offense, the principles of screening shall apply equally to the offense and defense.

INTERPRETATION

Play: A defensive player maneuvers to a position in front of post player A1 to prevent A1 from receiving the ball. A pass is made over the head and out of reach of the defensive player. Post player A1 moves toward the basket to catch the pass and try for goal. As the pass is made, a teammate of the defensive player moves into the path of A1, in a guarding position.

Ruling: This action involves a screening principle. The defensive player has switched to guard a player who does not have the ball. Therefore, the switching player must assume a position one or two strides in advance of the pivot player (depending upon the speed of movement of the pivot player) to make the action legal. When A1 has control of the ball (provided that the pivot player is not in the air at the time), the play shall become a guarding situation. When it is a guarding situation involving the player with the ball, time and distance shall be irrelevant.

Section 56. Shot Clock

Art. 1. A shot clock is one of the two official visible timepieces that display the amount of time the team in

control has to release a try for a field goal so that it hits
the ring or the flange.

INTERPRETATION

Play: There are 37 seconds (**men**) or 32 seconds
(**women**) on the game clock and 35 seconds (**men**)
or 30 seconds (**women**) on the shot clock. Team A
uses time before A1 releases the ball for a try for
goal. After A1 releases the ball, the shot-clock horn
sounds. The ball does not strike the ring or the
flange and the official calls a shot-clock violation.
The official's whistle sounds at the same time as the
game-clock horn sounds to end the period. Shall
the official put two seconds back on the game
clock?

Ruling: No. The shot-clock horn sounded at the
expiration of the shot-clock period. However, this
does not stop play unless recognized by the official's
whistle. The official's whistle for the shot-clock violation stopped play. The expiration of playing time
was indicated by the official timer's signal, which
shall terminate player activity. The period shall end
with the violation.

Section 57. **Shot-Clock Try**

Art. 1. A shot-clock try for field goal is defined as the
ball having left the shooter's hand(s) before the sounding of the shot-clock horn and then striking the ring or
the flange, or entering the basket.

Section 58. **Shooter**

Art. 1. A shooter is a player who attempts a try for a
field goal or a free throw.

Section 59. **Substitute**

Art. 1. A substitute is a team member who has reported to the scorers' table that he or she wishes to become a player and is waiting at the scorers' table to be beckoned into the game by an official.

Section 60. **Tap**

Art. 1. A tap is a type of try for field goal whereby a player attempts to score two or three points by directing a live ball into his or her team's basket with his or her hands or fingers.

Art. 2. A tap shall start when the player's hand(s) or finger(s) touch the ball.

Art. 3. A tap shall end when it is successful, when it is certain that the tap is unsuccessful, when the ball touches the floor or when the ball becomes dead.

Section 61. **Team Member**

Art. 1. A team member is a member of bench personnel who is in uniform and is eligible to become a player.

Section 62. **Three-Second Lane**

Art. 1. The three-second lane is the area in the front court that is bounded by the end line, the free-throw lane lines and the free-throw line, and includes such lines.

Section 63. **Throw-in/Thrower-in**

Art. 1. A throw-in is the method of putting the ball in play from out of bounds.

Art. 2. A thrower-in is the player attempting the throw-in.

Art. 3. A throw-in and the throw-in count shall begin when the ball is at the disposal of the player entitled to the throw-in.

Art. 4. A thrower-in shall have five seconds from receiving disposal of the ball to release the throw-in. The throw-in count shall end when the ball is released by the thrower-in so that the ball goes directly into the playing court.

Art. 5. A throw-in shall end when the passed ball touches or is legally touched by an inbounds player other than the thrower-in.

Art. 6. After a goal is scored by an opponent or awarded because of basket interference or goaltending, the thrower-in may run along the end line.

Art. 7. A thrower-in shall be permitted to throw the ball to a teammate along the end line after a goal is scored by an opponent or awarded because of basket interference or goaltending.

Section 64. Traveling

Art. 1. Traveling occurs when a player holding the ball moves a foot or both feet in any direction in excess of prescribed limits described in this Rule.

INTERPRETATION

Play: A1 attempts a try at Team A's basket after having completed the dribble. The try does not touch the backboard, the ring, flange or any other player. A1 runs and catches the ball before it strikes the playing court. Is this traveling?

Ruling: When A1 recovered his or her own try, A1 could either dribble, pass or try again. There is no team control by either team when a try is in flight. However, when the shot clock expires and a try by A1 or a teammate has not struck the ring, it shall be a violation of the shot-clock rule.

Art. 2. A player who catches the ball with both feet on the playing court may pivot, using either foot. When one foot is lifted, the other is the pivot foot.

Art. 3. A player who catches the ball while moving or dribbling may stop and establish a pivot foot as follows:

a. When both feet are off the playing court and the player lands:

   1. Simultaneously on both feet, either may be the pivot foot;
   2. On one foot followed by the other, the first foot to touch shall be the pivot foot;
   3. On one foot, the player may jump off that foot and simultaneously land on both; neither foot can be the pivot foot.

b. When one foot is on the playing court:

   1. That foot shall be the pivot foot when the other foot touches in a step;
   2. The player may jump off that foot and simultaneously land on both; neither foot can then be the pivot foot.

Art. 4. After coming to a stop and establishing the pivot foot:

a. The pivot foot may be lifted, but not returned to the playing court, before the ball is released on a pass or try for goal;

b. The pivot foot shall not be lifted before the ball is released to start a dribble.

INTERPRETATIONS

Play 1: A1 receives a pass from A2 and comes to a stop legally with the right foot established as the pivot foot. A1 tosses the ball from one hand to the other several times and then proceeds to bat the ball to the floor before A1 lifts the pivot foot.

Ruling: Legal.

Play 2: A1 attempts to catch the ball while running. A1 fumbles the ball and succeeds in securing it before it strikes the playing court. A1 then

begins a dribble, taking several steps between the time A1 first touched the ball until catching it.
Ruling: There has been no violation provided that A1 released the ball to start the dribble before lifting the pivot foot from the playing court after catching the ball.

Art. 5. After coming to a stop when neither foot can be the pivot foot:

a. One or both feet may be lifted, but may not be returned to the playing court, before the ball is released on a pass or try for goal;
b. Neither foot shall be lifted, before the ball is released, to start a dribble.

INTERPRETATION

Play: Is it traveling when a player (a) falls to the playing court while holding the ball; or (b) gains control of the ball while on the playing court and then, because of momentum, rolls or slides, after which the player passes or starts a dribble before getting to his or her feet?
Ruling: In (a), yes, because it is virtually impossible not to move the pivot foot when falling to the playing floor. In (b), no. The player may pass, shoot, start a dribble or call a timeout. Once the player has the ball and is no longer sliding, he or she may not roll over. When flat on his or her back, the player may sit up without violating. When the player puts the ball on the floor, then rises and is the first to touch the ball, it also is traveling. When a player rises to his or her feet while holding the ball, a traveling violation occurs. When a player falls to one knee while holding the ball, it is traveling when the pivot foot moves.

Section 65. **Try for Field Goal/Act of Shooting**

Art. 1. A try for field goal is an attempt by a player to score two or three points by throwing or tapping the ball into his or her basket.

INTERPRETATIONS

Play 1: A1 becomes confused and shoots the ball at the wrong basket. A1 is fouled while trying to shoot and the ball goes in the basket. Is this a goal? If A1 missed, should A1 be granted two free throws for the foul by the Team B player?

Ruling: No goal. The ball became dead when the foul occurred. When a player shoots at the opponent's basket, it is not a try. When Team A is in the bonus when the Team B player fouls A1, A1 shall be awarded a one-and-one. When Team A is not in the bonus, the ball shall be awarded to Team A at the designated spot.

Play 2: A ball passed from behind the three-point line (a) enters the basket from above and passes through, (b) is deflected and enters the basket from above and passes through, (c) strikes the side of the ring.

Ruling: In (a) a three-point goal shall be counted. (b) When there is no possibility of the ball entering the basket from above and the deflection causes the goal to be successful, it shall be a 2-point goal. However, when a ball is passed in the direction of the basket with the possibility of entering the basket from above and the deflection does not influence its success, a three-point goal shall be counted. (c) The ball shall remain live.

Art. 2. The try shall start when the player begins the motion that habitually precedes the release of the ball on a try. The ball does not need to leave the player's hand. The arm might be held so that the player cannot throw; however, he or she may be making an attempt.

INTERPRETATION

Play: B1 commits a common foul by holding A1 during a field-goal try but after A1 has completed the act of shooting (see airborne-shooter exception for **men** in Rule 4-65.6). The foul occurs before the bonus. The attempt is: (a) successful or (b) unsuccessful.

Ruling: A personal foul shall be charged to B1 in both (a) and (b) but no free throw shall be awarded to A1 in either case. In both (a) and (b), the ball shall be awarded to Team A at a designated spot.

Art. 3. A try shall end when the throw is successful, it is certain the throw is unsuccessful, when the thrown ball touches the floor or when the ball becomes dead.

Art. 4. A dunk attempt is a try.

INTERPRETATION

Play: A1 intercepts a pass and dribbles toward A's basket for a break-away layup. Near A's free-throw line, A1 legally stops and ends his or her dribble. A1 throws the ball against A's backboard and follows the throw. While airborne, A1 rebounds the ball off the backboard and dunks.

Ruling: The play shall be legal since the backboard is equipment located in A1's half of the playing court, which A1 is entitled to use.

Art. 5. When the game clock displays 10ths of seconds and play is to be resumed by a throw-in or a free throw when 3/10 (.3) of a second or less remains on the game clock, a player may not gain possession of the ball and try for a field goal. Such player can only score a field goal by means of a tap of the pass or of a missed free throw.

INTERPRETATION

Play: With ⁷⁄₁₀ of a second remaining on the game clock, Team A is awarded a throw-in at the division line. A1 passes the ball to A2 who (a) catches the ball with both hands while in the air and throws the ball into his or her basket or (b) does not catch the ball but taps it into the basket. In both (a) and (b), the ball is in the air on the way to the basket when the game-ending horn sounds.

Ruling: In (a), the score shall not count. With ³⁄₁₀ (.3) of a second or less remaining on the game clock or shot clock, when the ball is to be put in play by a throw-in, a player can only tap the ball to score a field goal. Despite the ball being in the air before the game-clock horn sounded, the official shall disallow the basket. In (b), the basket shall count.

Art. 6. The act of shooting shall begin simultaneously with the start of the try and end when the ball is clearly in flight, including when the shooter is an airborne shooter.

INTERPRETATION

Play: A1 is in possession of the ball and in the act of shooting when (a) A2 is fouled by B1 or (b) A2 fouls B2 before the release of the ball.

Ruling: In (a), assess B1 with the foul committed against A2. A1's try for goal shall count when successful. Administer the bonus free throw or award the ball to Team A at the designated spot. In (b), assess A2 with the foul committed against B2.

A1's try for field goal shall not count when successful, since the ball became dead before A1's release. The official shall administer the bonus free throw or award the ball to Team B at the designated spot.

Exception (Men): *An airborne shooter who is fouled by an opponent while in the air but after the ball is released shall be considered to be in the act of shooting until one of the airborne shooter's feet return to the floor.*

Section 66. Uniform

Art. 1. A uniform shall consist of the game pants and game jersey. Game pants are the bottom portion of the uniform. Game jerseys are the top part of the uniform.

Section 67. Unsporting Conduct

Art. 1. Unsporting conduct is behavior or an act that is unbecoming to a fair, ethical and honorable individual.

Section 68. Verticality

Art. 1. Verticality applies to a legal position. The basic components of the principle of verticality are:

a. Legal guarding position must be established and attained initially, and movement thereafter must be legal.
b. From such position, the defender may rise or jump vertically and occupy the space within his or her vertical plane.
c. The hands and arms of the defender may be raised within his or her vertical plane while the defender is on the playing court or in the air.
d. The defender shall not be penalized for leaving the playing court vertically or having his or her hands and arms extended within the vertical plane.
e. The offensive player, whether on the playing court or airborne, shall not "clear out" or cause contact that is not incidental.

    f. The defender may not "belly up" or use the lower part of the body or arms to cause contact outside his or her vertical plane.

    g. The player with the ball shall be given no more protection or consideration than the defender in the judging of which, if either, player has violated the principle of verticality.

Section 69. Violation

Art. 1. A violation is a rules infraction of the type listed in Rule 9.

Section 70. Warm-Ups

Art. 1. Warm-ups are any pieces of clothing worn by team members that must be removed before they become players. Warm-ups shall not be considered part of the uniform.

Rule 5

Scoring and Timing Regulations

Rule 5

Scoring and Timing Regulations

Section 1. **Scoring**

Art. 1. A goal from the field other than from beyond the three-point line shall count two points for the team into whose basket the ball is thrown, tapped or directed.

INTERPRETATION

Play: A pass or a try for field goal by A1 comes down several feet in front of the basket. The ball strikes the playing court without touching any player and bounces into the basket. Shall two points be counted for Team A: (a) when not complicated by the expiration of time in a period or by a foul occurring while the ball is in flight; or (b) when time expires or a foul occurs while the ball is in flight?

Ruling: In (a), two points shall be scored. The try for field goal by A1 ends when the ball touches the playing court but a field goal can sometimes be scored when, technically, it is not the result of a try. The points shall count for the proper team. In the case cited, it is customary to credit the two points to A1. In (b), no points shall be scored. Neither the expiration of time nor a foul shall cause the ball to become dead immediately during a try for a field goal. During a pass, the ball shall become dead as a result of the foul or expiration of time. (See Rule 4-65.3.)

Art. 2. A successful try from beyond the three-point line shall count three points for the team into whose basket the ball is thrown or directed.

Art. 3. Whether the game clock is running shall have no influence on the counting of a goal.

Art. 4. A goal from a free throw shall be credited to the free-thrower and shall count one point for the free-thrower's team.

Art. 5. For **women**, when a player-control foul occurs after a goal, the goal shall be canceled.

Art. 6. When a player scores a field goal in the opponent's basket, it shall count two points for the opponent regardless of the location on the playing court from where it was released. Such a field goal shall not be credited to a player in the scorebook but shall be indicated with a footnote.

INTERPRETATION

Play: A2 receives the tap by A1 on the jump ball to start an extra period. A2 is confused and dribbles toward the basket that Team A had during the first half and (a) dunks into Team B's basket or (b) attempts a three-point try at Team B's basket, which is successful.

Ruling: In both (a) and (b), the goal shall be legal. Two points shall be awarded to Team B. The ball shall be awarded to Team A out of bounds at the basket of Team B, and Team A may put the ball in play from anywhere at the end line as after any score by Team B (earned or awarded).

Art. 7. The only infractions for which points are awarded are goaltending by the defense or basket inter-ference at the opponent's basket.

Section 2. **Winning Team**

Art. 1. The winning team shall be the team that has accumulated the greater number of points when the game ends, except in Rule 5-3.2.

Section 3.   **Forfeit**

Art. 1. When a forfeit is declared, the score shall be recorded as 2-0 and all statistics (other than the teams' and coaches' won-lost records) shall be voided, unless 30 minutes of playing time has been completed on the game clock. In that case, the score at the end of play shall stand and all other statistics shall count.

Art. 2. When the team that is behind in the scorebook is to be declared the winning team, that score shall be marked with an asterisk in the official statistics; and it shall be noted that the game was won by forfeit.

Section 4.   **Interrupted Games**

Art. 1. When a game is interrupted because of events beyond the control of the responsible administrative authorities, it shall be continued from the point of interruption unless the teams agree otherwise or there are applicable conference, league or association rules.

Section 5.   **Protests**

Art. 1. The NCAA Men's and Women's Basketball Rules Committees do not recognize or allow protests.

Section 6.   **Length of Periods**

Art. 1. Playing time for varsity games shall consist of two halves of 20 minutes each with a halftime intermission of 15 minutes. Extra periods shall be five minutes each in length with a one-minute intermission before each.

> ***Note:*** *For the NCAA men's and women's regional finals, national semifinals and championship games, the length of the intermission for halftime may be increased by five minutes.*

Art. 2. The length of periods for non-varsity games may be reduced by conference, league or association rules or by mutual agreement of both teams and the referee.

Section 7. **Beginning and End of Period**

Art. 1. Each period shall begin when the ball becomes live.

Art. 2. Each period shall end when time expires except that:

a. When the ball is in flight during a try, the period shall end when the try ends.

b. When a held ball or violation occurs so near the expiration of time that the game clock is not stopped before time expires, the period shall end with the held ball or violation.

c. When a foul occurs so near the expiration of time that the official timer cannot stop the game clock before time expires or when the foul occurs after time expires but while the ball is in flight during a try. The period shall end when the free throw(s) and all related activity have been completed.

   1. After the game-clock horn sounds to end the game, only those free throw(s) necessary to determine a winner or whether an extra period is necessary shall be awarded.

INTERPRETATIONS

Play 1: With a few seconds remaining on the game clock in the first half, A1 makes a throw-in to A2 (game clock not started—official timer's error). A2 dribbles into the front court and misses the try. B1 recovers the rebound and dribbles the full length of the playing court. As the player passes the bench, the coach of Team A notices that the game clock has not started and calls the error to the attention of the official timer, who starts the game clock. With one second left on the game clock in the half, A2 fouls B1. The bonus is in effect. Time expires before the official timer can stop the game clock. ***Ruling:*** Assess A2 with a personal foul. Administer the free throw(s) before the intermission. The referee cannot correct this official timer's error because the referee does not know exactly how much playing time elapsed while the game clock was stopped.

Play 2: With the score tied near the expiration of time in the second half (a) shooter A1 is fouled in the act of shooting just before time expires or (b) shooter A1 is fouled in the act of shooting after time expires.
Ruling: (a) When the foul occurs before the ball becomes dead and the period has ended, A1 shall shoot the two free throws. When one free throw is successful, the game is over. If one free throw is not successful, the game continues with an extra period(s). (b) When the foul occurs after the second half has clearly ended, the extra period shall begin with the free throws.

Art. 3. No penalty or part of a penalty shall carry over from one half or extra period to another.
Art. 4. When a direct or indirect technical foul occurs after the ball has become dead to end a period, the next period shall be started by administering the free throws and play shall resume at the point of interruption. This shall apply when the foul occurs after the first half has ended or after the second half or any extra period has ended, provided that there is to be an(other) extra period.

a. When there is no way to determine whether there will be an extra period until the free throws for a technical foul are administered, the free throws shall be attempted immediately, as if the technical foul had been part of the preceding period.

INTERPRETATION

Play: Time for the first half expires while the ball is in flight during a field-goal try by A1. B1 intentionally fouls A2 before the field-goal attempt has ended. After the ball has become dead and after the last free throw by A2, A3 flagrantly fouls B1.
Ruling: A3 shall be ejected. Because the foul by A3 was committed after the first half expired, the second half shall begin with the free throws by any Team B player(s). The foul by A3 shall be considered to have been committed between the first and second halves.

Section 8. **Extra Period**

Art. 1. When the score is tied at the end of the second half, play shall continue without change of baskets for one or more extra period(s) with a one-minute intermission before each extra period. The game shall end when, at the end of any extra period, the score is not tied.

Art. 2. The length of each extra period shall be five minutes. As many such periods as are necessary to break the tie shall be played.

Art. 3. Each extra period is an extension of the second half.

Section 9. **Stopping Game and Shot Clocks**

The game clock and shot clock, if running, shall be stopped when an official . . .

Art. 1. Signals:

a. A foul.

b. A held ball.

c. A violation.

Art. 2. Stops play:

a. Because of an injury.

b. To confer with the scorers, timer or shot-clock operator.

c. Because of unusual delay in a dead ball being made live.

d. For any emergency.

Art. 3. Grants a player's visual or oral request for a timeout, such request being granted when:

a. The ball is in control or at the disposal of a player of his or her team. ***Exception:*** No timeout may be granted during an interrupted dribble.

b. The ball is dead (after the throw-in starts, no timeout shall be granted to the opponents of the throw-in team).

c. A disqualified or injured player(s) has been replaced when a substitute(s) is available.

Art. 4. Grants a coach's request for a timeout, such request being granted only when the coach's team is in possession of the ball (this includes throw-ins and free throws) or when the ball is dead. The official must be certain the request was made by a coach (head coach for **men**).

Art. 5. Recognizes a request by a coach (head coach for **men**) or player for a timeout after a goal until a player on the team putting the ball in play from the end line is positioned out of bounds with the ball.

Art. 6. Responds to the official scorer's signal to grant a head coach's request to address the possibility of a correctable error as in Rule 2-10 or whether a timing, scoring or alternating-possession mistake needs to be prevented or rectified. The appeal to the official shall be presented at the scorers' table, where a coach of each team may be present.

Art. 7. Suspends play immediately when necessary to protect an injured player.

INTERPRETATION

Play: When an official on his or her own initiative takes a timeout to protect an injured player, should a timeout be charged to the team?

Ruling: After calling the timeout, the official should ask the player if the player desires a timeout. When the player does not, play should be resumed immediately. When the player is not ready to resume play immediately and is not replaced until at least the next opportunity to substitute after the game clock has started, one timeout shall be charged to the injured player's team. No official has the authority to charge a timeout to himself or herself. (See Rule 5-9.2.a.)

Art. 8. Suspends play after the ball is dead or controlled by the injured player's team or when the opponents complete a play after a player is injured.

a. A play shall be completed when a team loses immediate control (including trying for goal) or withholds the ball from play by ceasing to attempt to score or advance the ball to a scoring position.

Art. 9. Suspends play when a player incurs a wound that causes bleeding or has blood on his or her body caused by blood from another player's wound. The official shall stop the game at the earliest possible time and instruct the player to leave the game for attention by medical personnel.

a. A player with blood on his or her uniform shall have the uniform evaluated by medical personnel. When medical personnel determines that the blood has not saturated the uniform, the player may immediately resume play without leaving the game. When medical personnel determines that the blood has saturated the uniform, the affected part of the uniform shall be changed before the player shall be permitted to return.

INTERPRETATION

Play: While Team A is dribbling, the referee notices blood on A1's game jersey. The referee blows the whistle to stop play. A1 goes to the bench and medical personnel (a) determine that the game jersey is not saturated with blood or (b) determine that the game jersey is saturated with blood.

Ruling: In (a), A1 may remain in the game without penalty. In (b), A1 shall leave the game and change to a blood-free game jersey. A1 shall remain on the sideline until the next opportunity to substitute or Team A may use a timeout to allow A1 time to change the game jersey. A1 may return to the game at the end of the timeout.

Art. 10. Recognizes each successful field goal in the last minute of the second half and the last minute of any extra period. Substitution shall not be allowed during these dead-ball situations.

Section 10.   Charged Timeouts

Art. 1. Time shall be out and the game clock and shot clock, if running, shall be stopped when:

a. A player or any coach (**women**) or a player or the head coach (**men**) requests a timeout, such request being granted only when the player's/coach's team is in possession of the ball (this includes throw-ins and free throws) or when the ball is dead.

INTERPRETATION

Play: Both teams remain in their huddles after a timeout even though the official administering the throw-in has alerted them that play shall resume. (a) Before or (b) after the ball is placed at the designated spot, Team A or Team B indicates it desires a timeout.

Ruling: In (a), either team may request and be granted a timeout. In (b), only the team entitled to the throw-in shall be granted a timeout after the throw-in count has started.

b. An injured player or a player who is bleeding or has a uniform that is saturated with blood has that condition remedied and is permitted to remain in the game.

Art. 2. In games not involving electronic media and also those with typed Internet coverage but **without** audio or video broadcast, the timeout format shall be:

a. Four 75-second timeouts and two 30-second timeouts for each team per regulation game.

b. The four 75-second timeouts may be used at any time.

c. The two 30-second timeouts may be used at any time.

d. When there is an extra period(s), each team shall be entitled to one extra 75-second timeout per extra period in addition to any timeouts it has not used previously.

e. Cheerleaders and mascots are permitted on the playing court only during a full timeout or an intermission.

f. Bands/amplified music are permitted to play or be played only during any timeout or intermission.

Art. 3. In games involving electronic media (i.e., radio, television, or Internet audio or visual broadcast), when the electronic-media format calls for at least three electronic-media timeouts in either half, the following shall be in effect: (TELEVISION, RADIO OR INTERNET AUDIO OR VISUAL BROADCAST MUST BE PRESENT TO USE THIS ELECTRONIC-MEDIA TIMEOUT FORMAT.)

a. When television is employed, there shall be four electronic-media timeouts in each half. These electronic-media timeouts shall occur at the first dead ball after the 16-, 12-, 8- and 4-minute marks.

> 1. The first 30-second timeout requested by either team in the second half shall become the length of a timeout called for by the electronic-media agreement.

b. When radio or Internet audio or visual broadcast is being used, electronic-media timeouts shall occur at the first dead ball after the 16-, 12-, 8- and 4-minute marks or after the 15-, 10- and 5-minute marks, depending on the electronic-media agreement.

> 1. The first 30-second timeout requested by either team in the second half shall be 75 seconds long or longer when called for by the electronic-media agreement.

2. When the electronic-media agreement calls for fewer than three electronic-media timeouts in one half, these electronic-media timeouts shall occur at the first dead ball after the minute marks specified by the electronic-media agreement.

c. Each team shall be entitled to four timeouts, 30 seconds each in length.

d. Each team may carry up to three 30-second timeouts into the second half.

e. Each team shall be entitled to one 60-second time-out that may be used any time during the game.
   1. No conference shall be permitted to extend the 60-second timeout by electronic-media agreement in electronic-media games.

f. A player or a coach from the same team may request successive 30-second timeouts.
   1. When these successive timeouts are granted, players shall be allowed to sit on their bench.

   2. When successive 30-second timeouts are granted, a warning horn shall be sounded 15 seconds before the expiration of the final 30-second timeout.

g. Unused 30-second team timeouts from the second half may be used in extra period(s).

h. A team-called 30-second timeout (excluding the first timeout of the game that becomes an electronic-media timeout) or the 60-second timeout in a game involving electronic media can be shortened when the captain/coach notifies the official of the team's intent to do so.

   1. When a request has been made to shorten a timeout for a purpose other than a substitution(s), a warning signal shall be sounded immediately and 15 seconds later a game-clock horn shall be sounded to resume play.

   2. When a request is made to shorten any timeout for a substitution(s), the signal for shortening a timeout shall be given and play shall be resumed immediately.

i. Each team shall be entitled to one additional 30-second timeout during each extra period.

    1. The first 30-second timeout requested in any extra period may become an electronic-media timeout when called for by the electronic-media agreement.

j. Cheerleaders and mascots are permitted onto the playing court only during an electronic-media timeout or intermission.

k. Bands and amplified music are permitted to play or be played only during any timeout or intermission.

Art. 4. When the electronic-media agreement calls for fewer than three electronic-media timeouts in one half, the format shall be as follows:

a. Four 75-second timeouts and two 30-second timeouts for each team per regulation game.

b. The four 75-second timeouts can be used at any time.

c. The two 30-second timeouts can be used at any time.

d. When there is an extra period(s), each team is entitled to one extra 75-second timeout per extra period in addition to any timeouts it has not used previously.

e. When the electronic-media agreement calls for either two or one timeout(s) in either half, those timeouts shall occur at the first dead ball after the minute mark specified in the electronic-media agreement. When either of the teams uses a 75-second timeout(s) in either the first or second half, that timeout shall replace the next agreed-upon electronic-media timeout(s) for that half.

Art. 5. In games involving electronic media, when a foul is committed that causes the ball to become dead at one of the specified time marks on the game clock for electronic-media timeouts, the free throw(s) shall be administered and the electronic-media timeout shall occur at the next dead ball.

Art. 6. When a 30-second timeout is charged for an injury, a bleeding player, a player's uniform that is saturated with blood or a correctable error, and it is the first 30-second timeout granted during the second half of the game, that timeout shall become an electronic-media timeout.

Art. 7. When a 30-second timeout is charged for an injury, a bleeding player, a player's uniform that is saturated with blood or a correctable error, and that timeout is granted at the first dead ball at one of the specified time marks on the game clock for electronic-media timeouts, that timeout shall become an electronic-media timeout.

Art. 8. A single charged full timeout in games not involving electronic media shall not exceed 75 seconds.

Art. 9. A single charged full timeout in a game involving electronic media shall not exceed 60 seconds.

Art. 10. A single charged 30-second timeout shall not exceed 30 seconds.

Art. 11. Only one 75-second timeout, in games not involving electronic media, or either one 30-second timeout or 60-second timeout, in games involving electronic media, shall be charged in Rule 5-9.2.a, regardless of the amount of time consumed when an injured player remains in the game.

Art. 12. A warning signal to alert teams to prepare to resume play shall be sounded 15 seconds before the expiration of any charged or electronic-media timeout.

Art. 13. A second game-clock horn shall be sounded at the end of any charged or electronic-media timeout and play shall resume immediately.

Art. 14. Substitutions shall not occur after the warning signal to prepare to resume play until at least one live-ball period has occurred and the ball becomes dead.

Art. 15. During a 30-second timeout, players shall stand inside the boundary lines.

Art. 16. During any timeout, bench personnel and players shall locate themselves inside an imaginary rectangle formed by the boundaries of the sideline (including the bench), end line, and an imaginary line extended from the free-throw lane line nearest the bench area meeting an imaginary line extended from the coaching-box line.

Art. 17. Successive charged timeouts shall not be granted after the expiration of playing time for the second half or after the expiration of any extra period.

INTERPRETATION

Play: After the second half expires with the score tied, A1 is charged with a flagrant technical foul. Either Team A or Team B then requests and is granted a timeout. At the expiration of the timeout, B1 attempts the first free throw, which is either successful or unsuccessful. After the free throw, either Team A or Team B requests and is granted a timeout.

Ruling: Illegal. The second timeout is considered to be immediately after the first timeout.

Art. 18. The team that requests a timeout may shorten that timeout when the captain/head coach notifies the official of the team's intent.

a. When a request has been made to shorten any timeout for a purpose other than for substitution(s), a warning signal shall be sounded immediately and 15 seconds later another signal shall be sounded to resume play.

b. When a request is made to shorten any timeout for a substitution(s), the signal for shortening a timeout shall be given and play shall be resumed immediately.

Art. 19. A timeout shall be charged to a team for either length or fraction thereof consumed under Rules 5-9.4 and 5-9.5, regardless of the amount of time consumed.

Art. 20. One 75-second timeout, in games not involving electronic media, or either one 30-second timeout or 60-second timeout, in games involving electronic media, shall be charged to the team making the appeal in Rule 5-9.6, when no correction is made or when the time limit for correcting an error under Rule 2-10 expires.

INTERPRETATION

Play: Team A coach requests a timeout for an official to assess whether a correctable error has occurred. The error is (a) correctable or; (b) not correctable.

Ruling: In (a) when the error is correctable, no timeout shall be charged to Team A. In (b) when the error is not correctable, a timeout shall be charged to Team A. When any portion of that timeout remains after the review of the request has been conducted, Team A shall be entitled to use that time. When the review requires the length of a timeout or longer, play shall resume immediately from the point at which it was interrupted at a designated spot.

Art. 21. No timeout shall be charged when:

a. In Rule 5-9.2.a, an injured player is ready to play immediately or is replaced until at least the next opportunity to substitute after the game clock has started after his or her replacement.

b. In Rule 5-9.3, the player's request resulted from displaced eyeglasses or lenses.

c. In Rule 5-9.6, a correctable error or a timing, scoring, or alternating- possession mistake is prevented or rectified.

1. When the time limit for correcting an error under Rule 2-10 has expired, a 75-second time-out shall be charged to the offending team in a game without electronic media.

Section 11. Time is Out—Start Game Clock

Art. 1. After time has been out, the game clock shall be started when the official signals time in. When the official neglects to signal, the official timer shall be authorized to start the game clock unless an official specifically signals that time shall continue to be out.

Art. 2. When play is started by a jump ball, the game clock shall be started when the tossed ball is legally touched.

Art. 3. When a free throw is not successful and the ball is to remain live, the game clock shall be started when the ball is legally touched by or touches a player on the playing court.

Art. 4. When play is resumed by a throw-in, the game clock and shot clock shall be started when the ball is legally touched by or touches a player on the playing court.

Section 12. Excessive Timeout

Art. 1. Timeouts in excess of the allotted number may be requested and shall be granted at the expense of an indirect technical foul charged to the offending team for each taken.

Art. 2. A 75-second timeout in games not involving electronic media or a 30-second or the 60-second time-out in games involving electronic media shall be charged to and may be used by the team requesting the granted excessive timeout.

Rule 6

Live Ball and
Dead Ball

Rule 6

Live Ball and Dead Ball

Section 1. **Periods—How Started**

Art. 1. The game and each extra period shall start with a jump ball between any two opponents.

Art. 2. The second half shall start with the team that controlled the alternating-possession arrow at the end of the first half given disposal of the ball at the division line opposite the scorers' table.

Art. 3. After any subsequent dead ball, the only way the ball may become live is to resume play by a jump ball, by a throw-in or by placing it at the disposal of a free-thrower.

Art. 4. The ball shall become live when:
a. On a jump ball, the ball leaves the official's hand.
b. On a throw-in, the ball is placed at the disposal of the thrower-in.
c. On a free throw, the ball is placed at the disposal of the free-thrower.

INTERPRETATION

Play: On a jump ball, the ball shall become live when it leaves the official's hand, but the game clock shall not start until the ball is touched.

Ruling: Most jump-ball violations occur after the ball leaves the official's hand. If the ball did not become live until touched, these would be acts during a dead ball and, therefore, be different from most other violations. (See Rules 5-11.2 and 9-7.)

Section 2. **Held Ball—Alternating Process**

Art. 1. In held-ball situations, teams shall alternate taking possession of the ball at the designated spot.

Art. 2. The team that does not obtain control of the initial jump ball shall start the alternating process when the next alternating-possession situation occurs by being awarded the ball at the designated spot.

INTERPRETATIONS

Play 1: The referee tosses the ball for the opening jump ball. Immediately after the ball is touched by the jumpers, A2 and B2 tie up the ball.

Ruling: Since possession has never been established, the referee cannot use the alternating-possession arrow to award possession. The referee shall conduct another jump ball. The players who tied up the ball—in this case A2 and B2—shall jump.

Play 2: During the opening jump ball, A1 illegally catches the tossed ball. The referee blows the whistle and awards the ball to B1 at the designated spot. How is the alternating-possession arrow established?

Ruling: The first legal possession is by B1 on the throw-in. As soon as the throw-in by Team B ends, the direction of the alternating-possession arrow shall be changed to that of Team A.

Art. 3. Before the start of the second half, the direction of the possession arrow shall be changed (to account for the teams switching ends of the court), indicating that the team that the arrow favored at the end of the first half shall maintain that status to start the second half.

Section 3. **Alternating-Possession Situations**

Art. 1. The ball shall be put in play by the team entitled to the throw-in at the designated spot where:

a. A held ball occurs.

b. The ball goes out of bounds as in Rule 7-3.

    c. A double free-throw violation occurs.
    d. A live ball lodges on a basket support. ***Exception:*** During a throw-in, a live ball lodging on a basket support is a violation.
    e. The ball becomes dead when neither team is in control and no goal or infraction or end of a period is involved.
    f. Simultaneous personal fouls are committed by the opponents.
    g. A double personal fouls occur when there is no team control as defined in Rules 4-13.2 and 4-13.3. The throw-in (no team control) is an exception.

INTERPRETATION

Play: (**Men**) A1 drives to the basket and (a) the referee calls a player-control foul and an umpire calls a block or; (b) the referee calls a charge and an umpire calls a block.

Ruling: This is uncharacteristic of a double personal foul where one official adjudicates the obviously committed fouls against two opponents. In (a) and (b) the two officials disagree that the fouls occurred simultaneously. In (a) the alternating-possession arrow shall be used and the ball shall be awarded at the designated spot. When the ball is awarded to Team A, there shall be no reset of the shot clock; when the ball is awarded to Team B, the shot clock shall be reset. To award the ball to Team A with the expired time instead of using the alternating-possession arrow would be unfair, since one of the fouls in question may have been committed when A1 was in control of the ball. In (b) although the two officials disagree as to whether there was a charge or a block, the ball was released by A1. During a try in flight there is no team control. The alternating-possession arrow shall be used and the ball shall be awarded at the designated spot. Since there is no team control, there shall be a reset of the shot clock when the ball is awarded to either Team A or Team B.

Art. 2. The direction of the alternating-possession arrow shall be reversed immediately after an alternating-possession throw-in ends. An alternating-possession throw-in shall end when the throw-in ends (Rule 4-63.5) or when the throw-in team commits a throw-in violation.

INTERPRETATION

Play: Thrower-in A1 breaks the plane of the boundary line by extending the ball over the playing court during an alternating-possession procedure. B1 creates a held ball. The official awards the ball to Team A since the alternating possession for the throw-in did not end. Was the official correct?

Ruling: The official was correct. An alternating-possession throw-in ends when the throw-in ends or when the throw-in team violates provisions of the throw-in. A1 has five seconds to release the throw-in. The throw-in count shall end when the ball is released by the thrower-in so that the ball goes directly into the playing court. The throw-in shall end when a passed ball touches or is touched by an inbounds player. Breaking the boundary plane with the ball by extending the ball over the playing court is not a violation of the throw-in provisions but the act does cause the ball to become live.

Art. 3. The opportunity to make an alternating-possession throw-in shall be lost when the throw-in team violates the throw-in provisions.

Art. 4. A foul by either team during an alternating-possession throw-in shall not cause the throw-in team to lose the alternating-possession arrow.

INTERPRETATIONS

Play 1: Team B is entitled to a throw-in under the alternating process. An official or the official scorer makes an error and the ball is erroneously awarded to Team A for the throw-in.

Ruling: Once the ball touches or is touched by an inbounds player, this situation cannot be corrected; however, Team B shall make the throw-in when the next alternating process occurs. Team B does not lose its throw-in opportunity as a result of the error.

Play 2: Team A is entitled to a throw-in under the alternating process. Before the throw-in by Team A is completed, a foul is called on either Team A or Team B.

Ruling: The procedure for any fouls called shall not be affected by the alternating process. The foul shall be charged and penalized. Team A shall receive possession for the throw-in when the next alternating process occurs. Team A shall not lose its throw-in opportunity as a result of the foul.

Play 3: During the alternating process, Team A violates the throw-in provisions by (a) leaving the designated spot, or (b) failing to pass the ball directly into the playing court so that after it crosses the boundary line it touches or is touched by another player (inbounds or out of bounds) on the playing court before it goes out of bounds, or (c) consuming more than five seconds before the ball is released, or (d) carrying the ball onto the playing court, or (e) touching it in the playing court before it has touched another player, or (f) throwing the ball so that it enters the basket before touching a player.

Ruling: When Team A violates the throw-in provisions, it shall lose its turn for a throw-in under the alternating process. Team B shall make the throw-in on the next alternating process.

Section 4. **Position for Jump Ball**

Art. 1. For any jump ball, each jumper shall have both feet inside the half of the center circle that is farther from his or her team's basket.

Art. 2. Each jumper may face in either direction.

Art. 3. The referee shall toss the ball upward between the jumpers in a plane at right angles to the sidelines, to a height greater than either of them can jump and so that the ball will drop between them.

Art. 4. The ball shall be touched by one or both of the jumpers after it reaches its highest point.

Art. 5. When the ball touches the playing court without being touched by at least one of the jumpers, the official shall toss the ball again.

Art. 6. Neither jumper shall touch the tossed ball before it reaches its highest point, leave the center circle until the ball has been touched, catch the jump ball, nor touch it more than twice.

INTERPRETATION

Play: During a jump ball, jumper A1 touches the ball simultaneously with both hands and then again touches the ball simultaneously with both hands.

Ruling: Legal. Touching the ball with both hands simultaneously shall be considered touching the ball once; however, when one hand touches slightly in advance of the second hand, that shall be ruled as touching the ball twice.

Art. 7. The jump ball and these restrictions end when the ball touches one of the eight non-jumpers, the playing court, the basket, the backboard or when the ball becomes dead.

Art. 8. When the referee is ready to make the toss, a non-jumper shall not move onto the center circle or change position around the center circle until the ball has left the referee's hand.

Art. 9. None of the eight non-jumpers shall have either foot break the plane of the geometrical cylinder that has the center circle as its base, nor shall any player take a position in any occupied space until the ball has been touched.

Art. 10. Teammates shall not occupy adjacent positions around the center circle when an opponent indicates a desire for one of these positions before the referee is ready to toss the ball.

Art. 11. Players may move around the center circle without breaking the geometrical cylinder that has the center circle as its base after the ball has left the referee's hand(s) during the toss.

Section 5.   Dead Ball

Art. 1. The ball shall become dead or remain dead when:

a. Any goal is made.

b. It is apparent that the free throw will not be successful on a free throw for a technical foul or a false double foul or a free throw that is to be followed by another free throw.

c. A held ball occurs or the ball lodges on a basket support.

d. An official blows the whistle.

e. Time expires for a half or extra period.

INTERPRETATION

Play: A1 rises and grabs the rebound clearly outside of the cylinder and, while airborne, dunks. Both hands are on the ball and in the basket when the game-clock horn sounds to signify the end of the period.

Ruling: This shall be ruled no goal; however, when the ball leaves the hands of A1 before the game-clock horn sounds to signify the end of the period, the dunk shall be considered the same as a try in flight; and the goal shall count.

f. A foul occurs.

g. Any floor violation (Rules 9-3 through 9-13) occurs, there is basket interference or goaltending (Rule 9-15) or there is a free-throw violation by the free-thrower's team (Rule 9-1).

INTERPRETATION

Play: The ball is in flight during a try for field goal by A1 when time in a period expires. As time expires, the ball is on the ring or in the basket or is touching the cylinder when it is touched by: (a) A2; or (b) B1. The ball then goes through the basket or does not go through.

Ruling: In (a) or (b), the ball shall become dead when touched by anyone. However, when illegal touching is by B1, two points shall be awarded to A1 (three points shall be awarded to A1 when it is a three-point try). Whether the ball goes through the basket shall have no effect upon the ruling. (See Rules 4-60 and 9-15.)

Section 6.   Ball Does Not Become Dead

Art. 1. A live ball shall not become dead until the try in flight ends when:

a. An official's whistle is blown.

b. Time expires for a half or extra period.

c. A foul occurs.

Art. 2. A live ball shall not become dead when a foul is committed by an opponent of a player who starts a try for goal before a foul occurs, provided that time does not expire before the ball is in flight.

INTERPRETATION

Play: As the hand of A1 contacts the ball to tap it toward the basket, B1 fouls A1. The ball is not airborne from the hand of A1.

Ruling: The penalty for a foul on a tap is the same as the penalty for a foul on a try. When the tap is successful, one free throw shall be awarded. When the tap is unsuccessful, two free throws shall be awarded.

Art. 3. A live ball shall not become dead when the ball is in flight on a try for field goal or during a free throw when an opponent swings his or her arms or elbows excessively without making contact. When the shooter, tapper or his or her teammates commit this infraction, the ball shall become dead immediately.

Art. 4. While a free throw is in flight, the ball shall not become dead when:

a. An official blows the whistle

b. A foul occurs.

Rule 7

Out of Bounds and the Throw-in

Rule 7

Out of Bounds and the Throw-in

Section 1. **Out of Bounds—Player, Ball**

Art. 1. A player shall be out of bounds when he or she touches the floor or any object other than a player on or outside a boundary line. An airborne player's status shall be where he or she was last in contact with the floor.

INTERPRETATION

Play: A1 blocks a pass near the end line. The ball falls to the floor inbounds but A1, who is off balance, falls outside the end line. A1 returns, secures control of the ball, and dribbles.

Ruling: Legal. A1 has not left the playing court voluntarily and was not in control of the ball when leaving the playing court. This situation is similar to one in which A1 makes a try from under the basket and momentum carries A1 off the playing court. The try is unsuccessful, and A1 comes onto the playing court and regains control of the ball.

Art. 2. The ball shall be out of bounds when it touches a player who is out of bounds; any other person, the floor, or any object on or outside a boundary; the supports or back of the backboard; or the ceiling, overhead equipment or supports.

INTERPRETATIONS

Play 1: The ball rebounds from the edge of the backboard and across a boundary line. Before the

ball touches the floor or any obstruction out of bounds, it is caught by a player who is inbounds.
Ruling: The ball is inbounds.

Play 2: The ball touches or rolls along the edge of the backboard without touching the supports.
Ruling: The ball shall be live unless ground rules to the contrary have been mutually agreed upon before the game.

Play 3: A throw-in by A1 strikes B1 who is inbounds, rebounds from B1 directly into the air, then strikes A1 who is still out of bounds.
Ruling: A1 shall be considered to have caused the ball to go out of bounds. The ball shall be awarded to Team B at the designated spot.

Art. 3. The ball shall be out of bounds when it passes over the backboard from any direction.

Section 2. **Ball Caused to Go Out of Bounds**

Art. 1. The ball shall be caused to go out of bounds by the last player to touch or to be touched by the ball before the ball goes out, provided that it is out of bounds because of touching something other than a player who is out of bounds.

INTERPRETATIONS

Play 1: A1, while dribbling, touches a nearby chair or the scorers' table while A1's feet are inbounds.
Ruling: A1 is out of bounds because A1 touched an object that is out of bounds; hence, the ball shall be considered to have gone out of bounds.

Play 2: A ball passed by Team A touches an official and goes out of bounds.
Ruling: Team B's ball.

Art. 2. When the ball is out of bounds because of touching or being touched by a player who is on or outside a boundary, such player shall have caused the ball to go out of bounds.

INTERPRETATION

> *Play:* A1, while dribbling, touches B1, who is standing on a sideline.
>
> *Ruling:* A1 is inbounds; however, when the ball in control of A1 touches B1, the ball is out of bounds and shall be awarded to Team A at the designated spot.

Section 3.   Ball Touched Simultaneously/Officials' Doubt

Art. 1. Play shall be resumed by use of the alternating-possession arrow when the ball goes out of bounds and:

a. Was last touched simultaneously by two opponents, both of whom are inbounds or out of bounds.

b. When the officials are in doubt as to who last touched the ball.

Section 4.   Ball Awarded Out of Bounds

Art. 1. The ball shall be awarded out of bounds after:

a. A violation as in Rule 9 or a double violation.

b. The last free throw of a penalty for a technical foul. (*Exception:* Rule 8-4.3)

c. A field goal or a successful free throw for a personal foul as in Rule 8-4.1.a or an awarded goal as in Rule 9-15.

d. The ball becomes dead while a team is in control provided that no infraction or the end of a period is involved.

e. A player-control foul.

f. A common foul before the bonus rule goes into effect.

g. A held ball as in Rule 4-35.

h. A double personal foul, to the team in control or in possession of the ball for a throw-in.

Section 5. **Out of Bounds, Ball in Play from**

Art. 1. When the ball is out of bounds after any violation as outlined in Rules 9-3 through 9-15, an official shall place the ball at the disposal of an opponent of the player who committed the violation for a throw-in from the designated spot.

INTERPRETATION

Play: When an official is required to hand/bounce the ball to the thrower-in, is it the duty of the official to wait until both teams are ready before doing so?

Ruling: No. The purpose of the rule requiring the official to hand/bounce the ball to the thrower-in in situations other than after a timeout is to indicate clearly which team is entitled to the throw-in after the official has given the direction signal and other necessary information. Teams are expected to be ready for all normal play situations. When the official inadvertently indicates the wrong team for a throw-in and discovers the error before play is resumed, the official should withhold the ball from play to permit the players to re-deploy themselves. Officials should not permit unusual delays to allow a team to set up a scoring play in the front court or to permit a specific player to take the ball for a throw-in. (See Rules 2-8.13.b and 10-3.1.c.)

Art. 2. When the violation is on a throw-in, the new throw-in shall be from the same designated spot as that of the original throw-in.

Art. 3. After a dead ball, as listed in Rule 7-4.1.d, any player of the team in control shall make the throw-in from the designated spot.

Art. 4. After a player-control foul or after a common foul before the bonus rule takes effect, any player of the offended team shall make the throw-in from the designated spot.

Art. 5. After a goal as listed in Rule 7-4.1.c, when a common foul is committed before the bonus is in effect, the team not credited with the score shall make the throw-in per Rule 7-5.6.

INTERPRETATION

Play: Team B has scored a field goal, and A1 has the ball along the end line for a throw-in. Team A is not in the bonus. Before the throw-in by A1 (a) B1 fouls A2 inbounds, near A1 or (b) B1 fouls A2 at the division line or (c) B1 fouls A2 beyond the division line.

Ruling: In (a), Team A, the team not credited with the score, may make a throw-in from the end of the court where the goal was made and from any point outside the end line. In (b) and (c), the ball shall be awarded at the designated spot. (See Rules 4-63.6 and 7-5.6.)

Art. 6. After a goal as listed in Rule 7-4.1.c, the team not credited with the score shall make the throw-in from the end of the court where the goal was made and from any point outside the end line.

a. Any player of the throw-in team may make a direct throw-in or may pass the ball along the end line to a teammate behind the end line.

INTERPRETATIONS

Play 1: After a goal by Team B, Team A has the ball for a throw-in from the end of the playing court from where the goal was made. (a) B1 intentionally kicks the ball out of bounds along the sideline or; (b) B1 intentionally kicks the ball out of bounds along the end line from where the throw-in was attempted.

Ruling: In (a) the kick is a floor violation and the ball shall be awarded to Team A at the designated spot. In (b) the illegal act of intentionally kicking the ball victimizes Team A. Consequently, Team A shall retain the privilege to the throw-in from anywhere along the end line. In (a) and (b), the throw-in was not legally completed since the kick, an illegal act, is an exception to the ball touching or being touched by a player on the playing court. As a result, the shot clock shall not start. When this situation occurs in the last minute of the second half or an extra period, neither the game clock nor the shot clock shall be started because of the violation.

Play 2: Team A scores a field goal. Team B requests and is granted a charged timeout.
Ruling: When the timeout ends, Team B may make the throw-in from anywhere behind the end line. Team B shall not be required to make the throw-in from a designated spot. Team B's taking a timeout does not restrict this privilege of throwing in from anywhere behind the end line. The same applies to a timeout after a successful free throw.

Play 3: (**Men**) A1 drives for a layup. After the ball leaves A1's hand but before it goes through the basket, A1 charges into B1. A1's try is successful. Team B is not in the bonus. The out-of-bounds spot nearest to where the personal foul occurred is on the end line. When the ball is handed to the thrower-in for Team B, may this player move along the end line?

Ruling: Yes. Team B shall be permitted to put the ball in play from any point out of bounds at the end line where the basket was scored since Team B was not credited with the score. Although Team B is not in the bonus, designating a spot shall not be necessary.

Art. 7. After a direct or indirect technical foul, any player of the offended team may attempt the free throws and the ball shall be put back in play at the point of interruption.

Exception: (*Women*) *When an indirect technical foul is for excessive timeouts, the ball shall be put back in play by the offended team at the designated spot after taking its merited free throws.*

Art. 8. After an intentional technical foul or a flagrant technical foul, any team member of the offended team may attempt the free throws and the ball shall be put back in play by any player of that team from a designated spot at the division line at either side of the playing court.

Art. 9. After an intentional personal foul or a flagrant personal foul, any player of the team to whom the throw-in has been awarded shall make the throw-in from the designated spot.

Art. 10. After a successful goal, when an intentional personal foul or a flagrant personal foul is committed near the end line, the team not credited with the score shall be permitted to make the throw-in from any point outside of the end line after taking its merited free throws.

Art. 11. After a double technical foul, the ball shall be put in play at the point of interruption.

Art. 12. After a double personal flagrant foul or after a double flagrant technical foul, play shall resume from the point of interruption.

Art. 13. After a double intentional personal foul or double intentional technical foul, play shall resume from the point of interruption.

Art. 14. After a double personal foul, any player of the team to whom the throw-in has been awarded shall make the throw-in from the designated spot.

Art. 15. After a free-throw violation by the shooting team as listed in Rule 9-1, any opponent of the shooting team shall make the throw-in from the designated spot.

Section 6.   Throw-in

Art. 1. The throw-in shall start when the ball is placed at the disposal of a player entitled to the throw-in.

Art. 2. The throw-in count shall end when the ball is released by the thrower-in so that the ball goes directly onto the playing court.

Art. 3. The thrower-in shall release the ball within five seconds so that the pass goes directly into the playing court, except as provided in Rule 7-5.6.

INTERPRETATION

Play: Team A scores a field goal. B1 catches the ball as it goes toward the floor from the basket. B1 steps out of bounds, runs a short distance and throws the ball to B2, who is standing out of bounds with one foot on but not beyond the end line. B2 does not break the plane of the inside edge of the end line until the ball has crossed the plane on the throw-in.

Ruling: Legal throw-in.

Art. 4. Until the thrown-in ball crosses the plane of the sideline or end line:

a. The thrower-in shall not leave the designated spot;

b. No opponent of the thrower-in shall have any part of his or her person over the inside plane of the sideline or end line;

INTERPRETATION

Play: B1 makes contact with the ball being passed between A1 and A2 while they are out of bounds (see Rule 7-5.6).

Ruling: A defensive player shall not interfere with the ball not yet inbounded. Indirect technical foul on B1.

c. Teammates shall not occupy positions parallel to the nearest boundary line when an opponent desires a spot between the positions.

d. Teammates may occupy adjacent positions near the sideline or end line when the teammates take adjacent positions that are perpendicular to the sideline or end line.

Rule 8

Free Throw

Rule 8

Free Throw

Section 1. Positions During Attempt

Art. 1. When a free throw is awarded, an official shall take the ball to the free-throw line of the offended team.

Art. 2. After allowing reasonable time for players to take their positions, the official shall put the ball in play by placing it at the disposal of the free-thrower.

Art. 3. The same procedure shall be followed for each free throw of a multiple free throw.

Art. 4. For **men**, a maximum of six players (four opponents of the free-thrower and two teammates of the free-thrower) shall be permitted on the free-throw lane during a free throw. All other players shall be behind the free-throw line extended and behind the three-point field-goal line.

a. Within this limit, opponents of the free-thrower may occupy the third or fourth lane space when it is not already taken. A teammate of the free-thrower may occupy the third space when it is not already taken but may never occupy the fourth space.

Art. 5. (**Women**) A maximum of six players (four opponents of the free-thrower and two teammates of the free-thrower) shall be permitted on the lane. All other players shall be behind the free-throw line extended and behind the three-point field-goal line.

a. The bottom two lane spaces closest to the basket have been eliminated for use.

b. The first spaces above the block closest to the free-throw line are designated lane spaces on either side of the lane for opponents of the free-thrower. The next available spaces closer to the free-throw line are designated for teammates of the free-thrower. The last two available spaces on either side of the lane closest to the free-throw line are designated for opponents of the free-thrower.

c. Teammates of the free-thrower shall not occupy lane spaces designated for opponents of the free-thrower; opponents of the free-thrower shall not occupy lane spaces designated for teammates of the free-thrower.

Art. 6. During a free throw for a personal foul, (**men**) each of the lane spaces adjacent to the end line shall be occupied by one opponent of the free-thrower.

(**Women**) Each of the lane spaces above the block closest to the free-throw line shall be occupied by one opponent of the free-thrower.

Art. 7. (**Men**) The opponents of the free-thrower occupying the lane spaces adjacent to the end line shall be permitted to position themselves up to the edge of the block that is farthest from the end line.

(**Women**) The opponents of the free-thrower occupying the lane spaces above the block closest to the free-throw line shall be permitted to position themselves up to the edge of the block that is closest to the free-throw line.

Art. 8. (**Men**) A teammate of the free-thrower shall be entitled to the second adjacent lane space on each side and an opponent of the free-thrower shall be entitled to occupy either of the next two lane spaces on each side.

a. Only an opponent of the free-thrower shall be permitted to occupy the last (fourth) space on either side of the free-throw lane.

b. Players shall be permitted to move along and across the lane to occupy a vacant space within the limitations listed in this Rule.

INTERPRETATION

Play: (**Men**) During the first of two free throws by A1, B2 does not occupy the third lane space and A3 takes it. Before the ball is handed to A1 for the second try, B2 requests permission to occupy the third space. *Ruling:* Grant B2's request.

Art. 9. A player shall position one foot at the near proximity of the outer edge of the free-throw lane line. The other foot may be positioned anywhere within the designated 3-foot lane space.

Art. 10. Only one player shall occupy any part of a designated lane space.

(**Women**) Only the last lane space above the block closest to the free-throw line on each side must be occupied.

Art. 11. When the ball is to become dead regardless of whether the last free throw for a specific penalty is successful, players shall not take positions along the free-throw lane.

Section 2. Who Attempts

Art. 1. Personal fouls—The free throw(s) awarded because of a personal foul shall be attempted by the offended player, unless one of the conditions of Article 2 of this section is met.

INTERPRETATION

Play: A2 attempts a free throw that should have been taken by A1.
Ruling: When the attempt by A2 is due to a justifiable misunderstanding, there shall be no penalty. The error shall be corrected under Rule 2-10. When it is reasonable to believe that A2 knew that A1 was the designated shooter, a direct technical

foul for unsporting conduct shall be called. In such a case, the direct technical foul shall be administered and the game shall be re-started at the point of interruption.

Art. 2. Under the following conditions, the free throw(s) that were to be attempted by the offended player shall be attempted by that player's substitute unless no substitute is available, in which case any teammate shall attempt the free throw(s):

a. When the offended player must withdraw because of injury;

b. When the offended player is bleeding or has blood on his or her uniform or person.

c. When the offended player is disqualified.

INTERPRETATION

Play: A1 is fouled by B1 and appears to be injured as a result. An official suspends play at the proper time. Team A indicates it desires a timeout. At the expiration of the timeout, it is apparent that a substitute for A1 is not necessary. Before the signal is given to resume play, A6 reports and is beckoned onto the playing court by an official. A6 indicates that he or she is to replace A1, which would avoid a timeout being charged to Team A.

Ruling: A1 shall be required to attempt the free throw(s) unless an injury prevents A1 from doing so. A6 should not have been beckoned onto the playing court since substitutions shall not occur after the warning signal.

Art. 3. Technical fouls—The free throws awarded because of any technical foul may be attempted by any player on the offended team, including an entering player, who shall be designated by the captain of the offended team.

Section 3. 10-Second Limit

Art. 1. The try for goal shall be attempted within 10 seconds after the ball has been placed at the disposal of the free-thrower at the free-throw line.

Section 4. Next Play

Art. 1. After a free throw that is not followed by another, the ball shall be put in play by a throw-in:

a. As after a field goal, when the try is successful and is for a personal foul, other than an intentional or flagrant foul.
b. At the point of interruption when the free throw is for a direct or indirect technical foul.

> ***Exception: (Women)*** *When an indirect technical foul is for excessive timeouts, the ball shall be put back in play by the offended team at the point of interruption.*

c. By any player of the free-thrower's team from the designated spot for any flagrant personal foul or any intentional personal foul.

Art. 2. After the game-clock horn has sounded to end regulation time or an extra period, only the free throw(s) necessary to determine the winner or whether a(nother) extra period is necessary shall be awarded unless an infraction of the rules occurs during the officials' jurisdiction.

Art. 3. Play shall resume with the administration of the penalty for a personal foul after the penalty for the technical foul has been administered. (***Exceptions:*** A single intentional technical foul and a single flagrant technical foul. See Rule 7-5.8.)

Section 5. Ball in Play When Free Throw is Missed

Art. 1. When a free throw for a personal foul is unsuccessful, or when there is a multiple free throw for a personal foul(s) and the last free throw is unsuccessful, the ball shall remain live.

Art. 2. When there is a multiple free throw and both a personal and a direct or indirect technical foul are involved, the tries for the indirect or direct technical fouls shall be attempted and play shall resume at the point of interruption.

> ***Exception: (Women)*** *When an indirect technical foul is for excessive timeouts, the ball shall be put back in play by the offended team at the point of interruption.*

Art. 3. When the last try is for a flagrant personal foul, the ball shall be put back in play at the designated spot.

Section 6. **Ball in Play After False Double Foul**
Art. 1. After the last free throw after a false double foul (Rule 4-26.11), the ball shall be put in play as if the penalty for the last foul of the false double foul were the only one administered.

INTERPRETATION

Play: Team A is assessed a direct technical foul. Right after the official hands the ball to B1 at the free-throw line, B2 flagrantly pushes A2. The referee ejects B2.

Ruling: No players shall take positions along the free-throw lane for B1's two free throws or for A2's two free throws. After A2's two free throws, Team A shall be awarded the ball for a throw-in at a designated spot.

Art. 2. When the last foul is a double flagrant personal foul or a double intentional personal foul, the ball shall be awarded to the team entitled to the alternating-possession throw-in.

Section 7. **Ball in Play After False Multiple Foul**
Art. 1. After the last free throw after a false multiple foul (Rule 4-26.13), the ball shall be put in play as if the penalty for the last foul of the false multiple foul were the only one administered.

Rule 9

Violations
and Penalties

Rule 9

Violations and Penalties

Section 1. **Free Throw**
Art. 1. The try shall be attempted from within the free-throw semicircle and behind the free-throw line.
Art. 2. After the ball is placed at the disposal of a free-thrower:
a. The free-thrower shall release the try within 10 seconds and in such a way that the ball enters the basket or touches the ring or flange before the free throw ends.

INTERPRETATION

Play: A1, at the free-throw line to attempt a free throw, is handed the ball by an official, who starts a silent count. A1 strikes his or her knee or leg accidentally with the ball while bouncing it and the ball rolls toward the basket between the free-throw lane lines.
Ruling: The official shall sound the whistle at once, causing the ball to become dead. The official should caution the free-thrower, place the ball at the disposal of A1 and start a new silent count.

b. The free-thrower shall not purposely fake a try nor shall the free- thrower's teammates or opponents purposely fake a violation.
c. No opponent shall disconcert (e.g., taunt, bait, gesture or delay) the free-thrower.

INTERPRETATION

Play: The ball is at the disposal of free-thrower A1. B1, within the visual field of A1: (a) raises the arms above the head, or (b) after the arms have been extended above the head, alternately opens and closes both hands.

Ruling: When the official judges the act in either (a) or (b) to be disconcerting, the official shall assess a penalty. The burden not to disconcert shall be that of the free-thrower's opponents.

d. No player shall enter or leave a marked lane space.
e. The free-thrower shall not enter the semicircle. The free-thrower shall not leave the semicircle before releasing the free throw.

INTERPRETATION

Play: After a timeout, the official administering a free throw has alerted players that the game shall resume. The free-thrower is not ready.

Ruling: When A1 is in the semicircle and does not take the ball or is outside the semicircle, the ball shall be placed on the free-throw line and the official shall start the count. A violation shall result when the free throw is not attempted in 10 seconds or when the free-thrower enters the semicircle. When A1 is outside the semicircle, A1 shall not enter the semicircle. However, any player from Team A may request and be granted a timeout before the expiration of the 10-second time limit for shooting the free throw.

f. Players not in a marked lane space shall remain behind the free-throw line extended and behind the three-point field-goal line until the ball strikes the ring, flange or backboard, or until the free throw ends.
g. Players occupying any of the legal marked lane spaces on each side of the lane may break the verti-

cal plane of a lane-space boundary once the free-
thrower has released the ball. (See Rule 8-1.)

h. Players occupying a marked lane space may not
have either foot beyond the vertical plane of the
outside edge of any lane boundary or beyond the
vertical plane of any edge of space (2 x 36 inches)
designated by a lane space mark or beyond the vertical plane of any edge of the lane until the ball is
released by the free-thrower.

Art. 3. (Men) An opponent of the free-thrower shall
occupy each lane space adjacent to the end line during
the try.

(Women) An opponent of the free-thrower shall
occupy each lane space above and adjacent to the
block.

Art. 4. No teammate of the free-thrower may occupy
either of the legal lane spaces nearest the basket.

INTERPRETATION

Play: After a timeout, the official administering a
free throw has alerted players that the game shall
resume. Team B is not occupying the respective
legal bottom marked spaces for men or women.
Ruling: Once the ball is placed at the disposal of
A1, an automatic delayed violation shall be called
on Team B for not occupying the bottom marked
space on each side. However, any player from Team
A may request and be granted a timeout before the
expiration of the 10-second time limit for shooting
the free throw.

Section 2. Free-Throw Violation Penalties

Art. 1. When a violation is by the free-thrower or the
free-thrower's teammate only, no point shall be scored

by that free throw. The ball shall become dead when the violation occurs. For any violation or personal foul (common, intentional or flagrant), the ball shall be awarded at the designated spot.

INTERPRETATIONS

Play 1: Before a free throw by A1 is in flight, A3 steps into the free-throw lane, then A2 pushes B2. *Ruling:* The ball becomes dead when A3 violates the free-throw lane provisions; therefore, the pushing of B2 by A2 shall be ignored unless it is flagrant, unsporting or intentional. (See Rule 4-26.3 to 4-26.7.)

Play 2: Before a free throw by A1 is in flight, A2 pushes B2, then A3 steps into the free-throw lane too soon. The bonus is in effect for both teams. *Ruling:* The foul by A2 causes the ball to become dead immediately. A3 did not commit a violation because the ball became dead when A2 fouled. A1 attempts the free throw with no players on the lane. The foul by A2 is then penalized, creating a false double personal foul. After the one-and-one attempt by B2, play shall be resumed as though the last personal foul of the false double personal foul were the only one administered.

Art. 2. When a violation is by the free-thrower's opponent only:
a. When the try is successful, the goal shall count and the violation shall be disregarded;
b. When it is not successful, the ball shall become dead when the free throw ends and a substitute free throw shall be attempted by the same free-thrower under the same conditions as those for the original free throw.

Art. 3. When there is a simultaneous violation by each team, the ball shall become dead when the violation by the free-thrower's team occurs, no point shall be scored, and play shall be resumed from a designated spot by awarding the ball to the team entitled to the alternating-possession throw-in.

INTERPRETATIONS

Play 1: On a free throw by A1, B1 commits a lane violation. A1's free throw misses the ring and flange.
Ruling: Double violation; alternating-possession rule.

Play 2: A2 and B2 commit lane violations (double violation) during (a) the first free throw of a one-and-one by A1 or (b) the first of two free throws by A1 or (c) the last or only free throw.
Ruling: In (a) and (c), the free throw shall be canceled and the alternating-possession rule shall apply. In (b), the first free throw shall be canceled and the second free throw shall be administered normally.

Art. 4. When there is a lane violation by a teammate of the free-thrower and an opponent:

a. When the first violation is by the free-thrower's team, the ball shall become dead when the violation occurs, no point shall be scored and play shall be resumed from a designated spot by awarding the ball to the opponent of the team that committed the first violation.

b. When the first violation is by the opponent of the free-thrower's team and the try is successful, the goal shall count and the violation shall be disregarded. When the try is not successful, the ball

shall become dead when the free throw ends and a
substitute free throw shall be attempted by the same
free-thrower under the same conditions as those for
the original free throw.

INTERPRETATIONS

Play 1: A1 and B1 violated the lane lines simultaneously during A2's free throw.
Ruling: When the official is unable to discern
which player committed the first violation, the ball
shall be awarded at a designated spot to the team
entitled to the alternating-possession throw-in.

Play 2: (**Women**) On the first shot of a one-and-
one, A1 is shooting and B1 and B2 are occupying
the two lane spaces adjacent to and above the block.
A2 is occupying the next lane space on the left side
of the basket (as she faces it). B3 lines up in the next
lane space on the right side of the basket (as she
faces it). A1 shoots the free throw and misses.
Ruling: A violation shall be called on B3 for lining
up in a lane space that is designated for Team A. A1
shall repeat the one-and-one free throw.

Art. 5. The out-of-bounds article in Rule 9-2.1 and the
alternating-possession article in Rule 9-2.3 shall not
apply when the free throw is to be followed by another
free throw or when there are free throws by both teams.
Art. 6. In Rule 9-2.3, when a violation by the free-
thrower occurs after disconcertion, a substitute free
throw shall be awarded.

Section 3.   Ball Out of Bounds
Art. 1. A player shall not cause the ball to go out of
bounds.

Section 4. **Throw-in**

Art. 1. The thrower-in shall not:

a. Leave a designated spot.

b. Fail to pass the ball directly into the playing court so that after it crosses the boundary line, it touches or is touched by another player (inbounds or out of bounds) on the playing court before going out of bounds.

c. Execute a throw-in that lodges between the backboard and the ring or comes to rest on the flange.

INTERPRETATIONS

Play 1: During a throw-in by Team A, A1's (a) foot breaks the plane of the boundary line or (b) A1's hand(s) and the ball break the plane of the boundary line.

Ruling: No violation in either (a) or (b).

Play 2: Thrower-in A1 attempts deception by throwing the ball against the edge of the front face of the backboard, after which it caroms into the hands of A2.

Ruling: The edge and front face of the backboard are inbounds and, in this specific circumstance, shall be treated the same as the playing court; hence, the throw-in shall be legal.

d. Consume more than five seconds from the time the throw-in starts until the ball is released.

e. Carry or hand the ball to a teammate who is on the playing court.

f. Touch the ball in the playing court before it has touched another player.

g. Throw the ball so that it enters the basket before touching anyone, strikes the back of the backboard or its supports, passes over the backboard, or bounces into the playing court from a balcony or from the floor out of bounds.

Art. 2. No player other than the thrower-in shall:

a. Perform the throw-in or be out of bounds after a designated-spot throw-in begins.

b. Be out of bounds when he or she touches or is touched by the ball after it has crossed the vertical inside plane of the boundary line. Repeated infractions shall result in an indirect technical foul.

Art. 3. The opponents of the thrower-in shall not have any part of their person beyond the vertical inside plane of any boundary line before the ball has crossed that boundary line.

Section 5. Travel, Intentional Kick, Fist, Through Basket from Below

Art. 1. A player shall not travel or run with the ball, intentionally kick it, strike it with the fist or cause it to enter and pass through the basket from below.

Section 6. Double Dribble

Art. 1. A player shall not dribble a second time after the player's first dribble has ended, unless the player subsequently loses control because of:

a. A try for field goal.

b. A bat by an opponent.

c. A pass or fumble that has then touched or been touched by another player.

Section 7. Jump Ball

Art. 1. A player shall not violate Rule 6-4.

Art. 2. The toss shall be repeated when both teams simultaneously commit violations during a jump ball.

Art. 3. The toss shall be repeated when the referee makes a bad toss.

Section 8. Three-Second Rule

Art. 1. A player shall not be permitted to have any part of his or her body remain in the three-second lane for more than three consecutive seconds while the ball is in control of that player's team in his or her front court.

INTERPRETATION

Play: The ball is loose.
Ruling: The three-second count shall be in effect except during an interrupted dribble. The team that had control before the loose ball shall maintain team control until the opponent secures control.

Art. 2. Allowance shall be made for a player who, having been in the three-second lane for less than three seconds, dribbles or moves in to try for field goal.

a. The player shall not pass the ball instead of trying for goal.

Art. 3. The count shall not begin nor shall it be terminated during an interrupted dribble.

Section 9. 10-Second Violation

Art. 1. (**Men**) A player (and his team) shall not be in continuous control of a ball that is in his back court for 10 consecutive seconds.

INTERPRETATIONS

Play 1: (**Men**) A1 is in the back court and has dribbled for eight seconds when he passes the ball forward toward A2 in the front court. While the ball is in the air, going from back court to front court, the 10-second count expires.
Ruling: Violation. The ball shall be awarded to Team B at the designated spot nearest to where A1 was standing when he threw the ball.

Play 2: **(Men)** With A1 in his team's back court and while being pressured by B1 during an attempt to advance the ball, the official has reached a seven count on A1. At this point, while A1 is still dribbling, B1 touches the ball and it goes back toward B's basket. A1 retrieves the ball and continues to dribble.

Ruling: There has been no change in team control. The 10-second count shall continue.

Section 10. **Shot Clock**

Art. 1. The team in control shall attempt a try for field goal within 35 seconds for **men** and within 30 seconds for **women** after any player on the playing court legally touches or is touched by the ball on a throw-in or when a team initially gains possession of the ball from a jump ball, an unsuccessful try for field goal or a loose ball.

INTERPRETATION

Play: B1 blocks A1's try for goal and the shot clock expires. The shot-clock horn sounds (a) while the ball is loose on the playing court, or (b) while A2 gains possession of the ball, or (c) while the blocked try is in the air and the ball subsequently strikes the ring or flange or goes in the basket.

Ruling: In (a) and (b), Team A has committed a shot-clock violation because the try did not strike the ring or flange. In (c), the shot-clock horn shall be ignored and play shall continue with the shot clock reset upon possession by either team because A1 complied with the shot-clock rule when the try struck the ring or flange or entered the basket.

Art. 2. The try for field goal shall leave the shooter's hand before the expiration of the allotted shot-clock time, and the try subsequently shall strike the ring or flange or enter the basket.

INTERPRETATIONS

Play 1: A1 releases the ball on a try for goal. After the ball leaves A1's hand(s), the shot-clock horn sounds. The ball (a) hits the backboard and goes through the net; (b) hits the backboard and rebounds directly to A2 or B1 without hitting the ring or flange; or (c) hits the backboard, strikes the ring or flange and rebounds directly to A2.

Ruling: In (a), score the field goal. In (b), a shot-clock violation by Team A has occurred because the try did not hit the ring or flange. The referee shall sound the whistle, and the ball shall be awarded to Team B at a designated spot. In (c), there is no shot-clock violation because the try hit the ring or flange. The shot clock shall be reset when Team A establishes possession of the ball on the rebound.

Play 2: With the alternating-possession arrow favoring Team A and 20 seconds remaining on the shot clock, A1's try for goal lodges between the backboard and the basket support.

Ruling: Team A shall be awarded possession for a throw-in and the shot clock shall be reset.

Play 3: B1 blocks A1's try for goal and the shot clock expires. The shot-clock horn sounds while B2 has gained possession of the ball.

Ruling: The shot-clock horn shall be ignored, the shot clock shall be reset and play shall continue.

Section 11. Ball in Back Court

Art. 1. A player shall not be the first to touch the ball in his or her back court when the ball came from the front court while the player's team was in team control and the player or a teammate caused the ball to go into the back court.

INTERPRETATION

Play: A1 receives a pass in Team A's front court and throws the ball to his or her back court where the ball (a) is touched by a teammate, (b) goes directly out of bounds or (c) rests, rolls or bounces with all players hesitating to touch it.

Ruling: Violation when touched in (a). In (b), it is a violation for going out of bounds. In (c), the ball is live so that Team B may secure control. When Team A touches the ball first, it shall be a violation. The ball continues to be in team control of Team A. For **men**, the 10-second count shall start when the ball goes in the back court, while the 35-second shot clock shall continue to run. For **women**, the 30-second clock shall continue.

Art. 2. A player meets the conditions of Article 1 of this Rule by having the ball touch any part of his or her body voluntarily or involuntarily.

Art. 3. A pass in the front court that is deflected by a defensive player so that the ball goes into the back court may be recovered by either team.

Art. 4. A defensive player shall be permitted to secure control of the ball while both feet are off the playing court and land with one or both feet in the back court.

INTERPRETATION

Play: B1 (a) secures possession of a rebound from Team A's basket or (b) has the ball for a throw-in under Team A's basket. B1 is in the front court of Team A (in other words, the back court of Team B). B1 attempts a long pass down the playing court to teammate B2. A2, standing in Team A's front court close to the division line, leaps and intercepts a pass by B1, then lands in the back court of Team A with player control.

Ruling: In both (a) and (b), no violation has occurred. These are exceptions to the back-court rule. (See Rule 9-11.5.)

Art. 5. A player shall be permitted to be the first to secure control of the ball after a jump ball or throw-in while both feet are off the playing court and the player lands with one or both feet in the back court.

Section 12.   Elbow(s)

Art. 1. A player shall not excessively swing his or her arm(s) or elbow(s), even without contacting an opponent.

INTERPRETATION

Play: While A1's try for field goal is in flight toward Team A's basket, B1 violently swings arm(s) and elbow(s) but makes no contact with any Team A player.

Ruling: The official shall sound the whistle immediately; however, the ball shall not become dead until it is apparent whether the try is successful. When the try is successful, the basket shall count and the violation shall be ignored. When the try is unsuccessful, Team A shall be awarded the ball at the designated spot. When a teammate of A1 committed a violation as B1 did, the ball shall be dead immediately. The ball shall be awarded to Team B at a designated spot.

Art. 2. A player may extend arm(s) or elbow(s) to hold the ball under the chin or against the body.

Art. 3. Action of arm(s) and elbow(s) resulting from total body movement as in pivoting or movement of the ball incidental to feinting with it, releasing it, or moving it to prevent a held ball or loss of control shall not be considered excessive.

Section 13. Closely Guarded

Art. 1. Closely guarded violations occur when:

a. A team in its front court (**men**) or on the playing court (**women**) controls the ball for five seconds in an area enclosed by screening teammates.

INTERPRETATION

Play: Team A, while in possession of the ball, lines up four of its players side by side, just inbounds at a boundary line. The four players pass the ball back and forth to one another with their arms reaching out beyond the plane of the boundary line. The players are in (a) the front court or (b) the back court.

Ruling: In (a), after five seconds, a violation shall be called. In (b), the 10-second rule applies for **men**.

b. (1) (**Men**) A closely guarded player anywhere in his front court holds or dribbles the ball for five seconds. This count shall be terminated during an interrupted dribble.

(2) (**Women**) A player in control of the ball, but not dribbling, is closely guarded when an opponent is in a guarding stance within 6 feet. A closely guarded violation shall occur when the player in control of the ball holds the ball for more than five seconds.

Section 14. Floor-Violation Penalties
(Applies only to Rules 9-3 through 9-13)

Art. 1. The ball shall become dead or remain dead when a violation occurs. The ball shall be awarded to a nearby opponent for a throw-in at a designated spot.

Art. 2. When the ball passes through a basket during the dead-ball period immediately after a violation, no point(s) can be scored and the ball shall be awarded to an opponent at a designated spot. (See Rule 4-15.)

Section 15.   Basket Interference and Goaltending

Art. 1. A player shall commit neither basket interference nor goaltending.

Art. 2. The ball shall be considered to be within the basket when any part of the ball is below the cylinder and the level of the ring.

Art. 3. A player may have a hand legally in contact with the ball, when this contact continues after the ball enters the cylinder or when, in such action, the player touches the basket.

Section 16.   Basket-Interference and Goaltending Penalties

Art. 1. When the violation is at the basket of the opponent of the offending player, the offended team shall be awarded:

a. One point for basket interference or one point and an indirect technical foul for goaltending when during a free throw.

b. Two points when during a two-point field-goal try.

c.   Three points when during a three-point field-goal try.

Art. 2. The crediting of the score and subsequent procedure shall be the same as when the awarded score results from the ball going through the basket, except that the official shall hand/bounce the ball to a player of the team entitled to the throw-in.

Art. 3. When the violation is at a team's own basket, no points shall be scored and the ball shall be awarded to the offended team at a designated spot.

INTERPRETATIONS

Play 1: B1 touches the ball while a throw-in is in the cylinder.

Ruling: Basket interference. Team A shall be awarded two points. Team B shall be awarded the

---

ball for a throw-in, as after a goal scored, except that an official shall hand the ball to a player of Team B and the player or a teammate shall make the throw-in. (See Rule 7-5.1.)

Play 2: The ball is in flight during a three-point field-goal try by A1 when a period expires. After the expiration of time and while the ball is rolling on the ring, B1 taps it into the basket.

Ruling: Basket interference by B1. Three points shall be awarded to A1 because of the basket interference.

Play 3: The ball enters the basket during a field-goal try by A1. Before the ball is in flight for the try, A1 is fouled. A2 touches the ring while the ball is in the basket.

Ruling: Basket interference on A2. The goal shall be canceled. A1 shall be awarded two free throws because of the foul.

Art. 4. When the violation results from touching the ball while it is in the basket after entering from below, no points shall be scored and the ball shall be awarded to the opponent at a designated spot.

Art. 5. When there is a violation by both teams, play shall be resumed by awarding the ball to the team entitled to the alternating-possession throw-in at a designated spot.

Rule 10

Fouls
and Penalties

Rule 10

Fouls and Penalties

Technical Fouls

Section 1.   **Forfeiture**

Art. 1. The referee shall declare a forfeit when any player, squad member or bench personnel fails to comply with any technical-foul penalty or makes a travesty of the game.

Art. 2. The referee shall declare a forfeit when conditions warrant.

Art. 3. The referee shall declare a forfeit when a team refuses to play after being instructed to do so by an official.

Art. 4. The referee shall determine the length of time that shall elapse before a forfeit may be declared.

Art. 5. Conference policy may include an established time limit before a forfeit may be declared.

Section 2.   **Penalties Resulting in Ejection**

Art. 1. Anyone who is assessed a combination of any three technical fouls (either two indirect and one direct, one indirect and two direct, or one intentional technical and two indirect) shall be ejected.

Note: The indirect technical fouls that can be part of these combinations are defined in Rules 10-3.9 through 10-3.20.

Section 3.   **Indirect Technical Fouls**

The following shall result in an indirect technical foul being charged to a team or player:

Art. 1. Delay of game. A team shall not delay the game. Delay of the game shall include, when the game clock is not running:

a. Consuming a full minute by not being ready when it is time to start either half or any extra period;

INTERPRETATION

Play: Team A is not ready to take the playing court after the second warning signal sounds to indicate the end of the halftime intermission.

Ruling: The referee should ask the timer to start the device used to time timeouts. At the expiration of one minute, Team A shall be assessed an indirect technical foul for delay of game. Team B shall be awarded two free throws and play shall be resumed at the point of interruption. When Team A is entitled to the alternating-possession arrow, it shall not lose control of the arrow. This indirect technical foul shall not be charged to the head coach nor toward the team's bonus.

b. Failure to supply scorers with data per Rule 3-3;
c. Repeatedly delaying the game by preventing the ball from being promptly put in play, such as delaying the administration of a throw-in or free throw by engaging in a team huddle any place on the playing court.
d. Failing to remove chairs/stools immediately after the warning signal of any timeout and to complete cleanup before the final warning signal alerts all personnel that play is going to resume.
   1. One warning shall be given to a team that fails to comply; an indirect technical foul shall be assessed thereafter.

Art. 2. Starting lineup/squad list. A team shall not change its designated starting lineup or add to its squad list. (See Rule 3-3.)

a. Infractions shall be penalized when discovered during the time the rule is being violated.

Art. 3. Number of players. A team shall not have more than five players.

a. Infractions shall be penalized when discovered during the time the rule is being violated.

Art. 4. Excessive timeouts. A team shall not be granted excessive timeouts without incurring a penalty.

Art. 5. Substitution

a. A substitute shall not enter the playing court without reporting to the scorers, without the substitute's name appearing on the pregame squad list or without being beckoned onto the playing court by an official (unless during an intermission).

b. Substitutions between halves shall be reported to the official scorer before the signal that ends the intermission.

Art. 6. Musical instruments, amplified music, artificial noisemakers, laser pointers. The playing of musical instruments and/or amplified music and the use of artificial noisemakers while the game is in progress shall be prohibited. The use of laser pointers by fans, coaches and team members shall be prohibited.

a. The only time the game, once started, is not "in progress" is during a timeout or intermission.

Art. 7. Debris on court. Purposely throwing debris onto the playing court shall be prohibited once the officials' jurisdiction has begun.

Art. 8. Center circle/division line. The home team shall comply with the division-line and center-circle rules. (See Rules 1-4 and 1-5.)

INTERPRETATION

Play: Team A and Team B are playing each other on Team D's home court in a tournament hosted by Team D. Team C will play Team D immediately after A's and B's game. There is no continuous division line or center circle on the playing court.

Ruling: Neither Team A nor Team B shall be assessed an indirect technical foul but, when Team D plays Team C, Team D, when the situation still exists, shall be assessed an indirect technical foul to begin the game since it is the home team. Only the home team shall be responsible for having a center circle and division line on its home playing court. Team C will shoot one free throw and the game shall start with a jump ball.

Art. 9. Wearing a number that is identical to that of a teammate (this also applies to all squad members included in the list of names supplied to the official scorer, Rule 3-3).

Art. 10. Wearing an illegal number.

a. Such offender shall be penalized when discovered before the ball becomes live.

Art. 11. Wearing an illegal game jersey.

a. Penalize offender when discovered before the ball becomes live.

Art. 12. Grasping either basket during the officials' jurisdiction.

a. When the player is not, in the judgment of an official, trying to prevent an obvious injury to himself, herself or an official.

INTERPRETATION

Play: A1 dunks and in so doing grasps the ring with a free hand: (a) before the ball leaves his or her other hand; or (b) after the ball clears the net.

Ruling: In (a), for **men**, A1 shall be assessed with two indirect technical fouls, one for grasping the ring and the other for dunking a dead ball. For **women**, A1 shall be assessed an indirect technical

foul for grasping the ring. In (a), no goal shall be
scored. In (b), the goal shall count and A1 shall be
assessed an indirect technical foul for grasping the
ring.

Art. 13. (Men) Dunking or attempting to dunk a dead
ball before or during the game or during any intermission until jurisdiction of the officials has ended. This
applies to all squad members.

INTERPRETATIONS

Play 1: Team A is ahead by one point. The game-
ending horn sounds with the ball loose at the
division line. Clearly after playing time has expired,
A1 grabs the ball and dunks. The referee, who is
near the free-throw line, on his or her way to the
scorers' table to check/approve the final score, sees
this action by A1 and assesses an indirect technical
foul. Team A's coach pushes the referee after the
indirect technical foul is called. The referee ejects
the coach from the game and awards Team B four
free throws.

Ruling: The referee is correct. The officials'
jurisdiction does not end until the approval of the
final score. Until the officials' jurisdiction ends, an
official may call a technical foul, correct a
correctable error (Rule 2-10), or correct a
bookkeeping mistake by the official scorer.

***Play 2:* (Men)** Fifteen minutes before the game is
scheduled to start and during the warm-up, squad
member A6 dunks and is charged with the
infraction. In defiance, A6 dunks a second and
third time.

Ruling: Team B shall be awarded six free throws
and A6 shall be disqualified.

Play 3: A1 is dribbling toward the basket and contact is made by B1 immediately before the start of the act of dunking. A1 continues the attempt to dunk.

Ruling: When the official sounds the whistle and calls a foul on either A1 or B1, the basket shall not count. For **men**, A1 shall not be assessed an indirect technical foul for dunking a dead ball, as long as the official believes there was reasonable doubt that A1 heard the whistle or that he could not react quickly enough to stop the dunk.

Play 4: A1 is in the act of dunking, and a foul is called on B2 or B1 off the ball.

Ruling: When A1 has started the throwing motion, the goal, when successful, shall count. For **men**, no indirect technical foul shall be called on A1 for dunking. When the foul off the ball is committed before A1 starts his throwing motion, the official still shall not call an indirect technical foul on A1 for dunking a dead ball when there is reasonable doubt that A1 heard the whistle. The referee shall not count the basket and shall penalize for the foul that was committed off the ball. (See Rule 10-3.12.)

Art. 14. Intentionally slapping or striking the backboard or causing either the backboard or ring to vibrate while the ball is in flight during a try, or while the ball is touching the backboard, is on or in the basket or in the cylinder.

Art. 15. Placing a hand(s) on the backboard to gain an advantage.

Art. 16. Deceptively leaving the playing court for an unauthorized reason and returning.

INTERPRETATIONS

Play 1: Team A sets a double screen for A1, who in attempting to come across the free-throw lane, is legally obstructed by offensive and defensive players so that A1 leaves the playing court under the basket, circles around, returns to the playing court and then receives the ball.

Ruling: An indirect technical foul shall be charged to A1 for deceptively leaving the playing court for an unauthorized reason and returning. Whether A1 receives the ball shall have no bearing on the decision.

Play 2: A player steps out of bounds to avoid contact.

Ruling: This shall not be called an indirect technical foul unless the player leaves the playing court to deceive in some way. When the player is a dribbler, the ball shall be ruled out of bounds.

Art. 17. Purposely delaying his or her return to the playing court after being legally out of bounds.

Art. 18. Attempting to gain an advantage by interfering with the ball after a goal by failing to immediately pass the ball to the nearest official when in control after a violation is called.

Art. 19. Touching a ball in flight during a free throw.

Art. 20. Delaying the game by preventing the ball from being promptly made live or by preventing continuous play.

INTERPRETATION

Play: After a field goal by B1 with two minutes left to play: (a) B2 reaches through the end-line plane and slaps the ball from the hands of A1 or touches the ball as it is passed along the end line after the score; or (b) after a warning, B2 prevents the ball from being promptly put in play by slapping the ball away.

Ruling: In (a) and (b), an indirect technical foul shall be charged to B2 for delaying the game. When A1, in making the throw-in, reaches through the end-line plane into the playing court and B1 slaps the ball from the hands of A1, without B1 breaking the plane above the end line, the ball becomes live and B1 has not committed a violation.

Section 4. Penalty for Indirect Technical Fouls

Art. 1. The penalty for indirect technical fouls shall be two free throws. The ball shall be put back in play at the point of interruption.

Exception: **(Women)** *An indirect technical foul for excessive timeouts shall carry the additional penalty of loss of possession.*

Art. 2. Indirect technical fouls shall not count toward a player's five fouls for disqualification or toward the team-foul total.

Art. 3. When double indirect technical fouls are committed before the start of the game, no free throws shall be awarded. The game shall begin with a jump ball.

Art. 4. When double indirect technical fouls are committed during a game, no free throws shall be awarded and play shall resume at the point of interruption.

Art. 5. A player who receives a combination of three indirect technical fouls, as described in Rules 10-3.9 through 10-3.20, and direct technical fouls shall be ejected.

Section 5. Direct Technical Fouls for Unsporting Player Conduct

Unsporting acts of players include, but are not limited to, the following:

Art. 1. Disrespectfully addressing or contacting an official or gesturing in such a manner as to indicate resentment.

Art. 2. Using profanity or vulgarity; taunting, baiting or ridiculing another player or bench personnel; or pointing a finger at or making obscene gestures toward another player or bench personnel.

Art. 3. Purposely obstructing an opponent's vision by waving or placing hand(s) near his or her eyes.

Art. 4. Climbing on or lifting a teammate to secure greater height.

Art. 5. Knowingly attempting a free throw to which he or she is not entitled.

Art. 6. Accepting a foul that should be charged to a teammate.

Art. 7. Inciting undesirable crowd reaction.

Art. 8. Using tobacco.

Section 6. Penalty for Direct Technical Fouls Involving Unsporting Conduct of Players

Art. 1. The penalty for direct technical fouls involving unsporting conduct of players shall be two free throws. The ball shall be put back in play at the point of interruption.

Art. 2. The direct technical fouls described in Section 5 of this Rule shall count toward a player's five fouls for disqualification and toward the team-foul total.

Art. 3. When double direct technical fouls are committed, no free throws shall be awarded. Play shall resume at the point of interruption.

Art. 4. Two direct technical fouls assessed to a squad member shall result in ejection of the offender.

Section 7. Direct Technical Fouls for Unsporting Conduct of Bench Personnel and Followers

Any bench personnel or followers of a team shall be assessed a direct technical foul for the following unsporting conduct:

Art. 1. Disrespectfully addressing an official.

INTERPRETATION

Play: The official is advancing up the playing court to cover the play and as the official passes Team A's bench with his or her back to it, someone on that bench uses uncomplimentary language. The official is certain from which bench the uncomplimentary language came but not from which party.

Ruling: When the official cannot, with assurance, determine the violator, the official shall charge the direct technical foul to the head coach. The official alone shall decide to whom a direct technical foul shall be charged. It is not the prerogative of the coach or other bench personnel to come forward as the party guilty of unsporting bench decorum.

Art. 2. Attempting to influence an official's decision.

Art. 3. Using profanity or language that is abusive, vulgar or obscene.

INTERPRETATION

Play: A1 is driving toward the basket when an official, while trailing the play and advancing in the direction in which the ball is being advanced, is sworn at by the coach of Team B.

Ruling: The official shall withhold the whistle until A1 has either made or missed the layup. The official then shall sound the whistle and assess the offending coach a direct technical foul, which could be flagrant.

Art. 4. Taunting or baiting an opponent.

Art. 5. Objecting to an official's decision by rising from the bench or using gestures.

Art. 6. Inciting undesirable crowd reactions.

Art. 7. Entering the playing court unless done with the permission of an official to attend to an injured player (see exceptions under bench-area restrictions).

Art. 8. Failing to replace a disqualified or injured player within 30 seconds when a substitute is available.

INTERPRETATION

> *Play:* A4 is disqualified from receiving his or her fifth foul. The coach of Team A does not have a substitute ready to enter the game after the permitted 30 seconds.
>
> *Ruling:* The referee shall blow the whistle and call a direct technical foul on Team A. This direct technical foul shall be assessed to the head coach and shall be one of the two direct technical fouls that the head coach can accrue before being ejected. Team A's substitute shall enter the game. Team B shall shoot two free throws and the ball shall be put back in play at the point of interruption.

Art. 9. Using tobacco.

Art. 10. Refusing to occupy the team bench to which the team was assigned.

Art. 11. Using electronic transmission (e.g., headsets, cellular telephones, modular telephones) to and from the bench area and using television monitors or replay equipment at court-side for coaching purposes.

INTERPRETATION

> *Play:* The referee notices that the head coach of Team A is using electronic transmission (e.g., headsets, cellular telephones, modular telephones) to

communicate with someone in the stands. This is discovered (a) before the start of the game or (b) during the game.

Ruling: In (a), the official asks the coach to remove the headset and discontinue using it. In (b), a direct technical foul shall be assessed.

Section 8. Penalty for Unsporting Conduct of Bench Personnel and Followers

Art. 1. The penalty for a direct technical foul involving unsporting conduct of bench personnel or followers shall be two free throws. The ball shall be put back in play at the point of interruption.

Art. 2. The bench direct technical fouls in Section 7 of this Rule shall count toward a substitute's five fouls toward disqualification (even though the team member is not participating in the game at that moment) and toward the team-foul total.

Art. 3. When double direct technical fouls are committed, no free throws shall be awarded. The ball shall be put back in play at the point of interruption.

Art. 4. All of the direct technical fouls mentioned in Section 7 of this Rule shall be charged to the offender, charged/assessed to the head coach or co-head coaches and shall count toward the team-foul total.

Art. 5. Two direct technical fouls assessed to bench personnel shall result in ejection of the offender.

Art. 6. The head coach or co-head coaches shall be ejected after (a) two direct technical fouls have been assessed to him, her or them, (b) three bench direct technical fouls have been charged to his or her team or (c) a combination of one direct technical foul and two bench technical fouls have been assessed to him, her or them.

Art. 7. An assistant coach who replaces the ejected head coach shall not inherit any direct technical fouls the head coach had accumulated. However, the assistant coach shall be responsible for direct technical fouls previously assessed to him or her in that game.

Section 9. **Bench-Area Restrictions**

Art. 1. All bench personnel except the head coach shall remain seated on the bench while the ball is live except to react spontaneously to an outstanding play, immediately sitting down on the bench afterward.

INTERPRETATIONS

Play 1: A team has co-head coaches.

Ruling: Before the start of the game, the team shall designate who the coach with "standing" privileges shall be. Both coaches shall be assessed all direct technical fouls.

Play 2: The head coach of Team A is standing within the coaching box to coach his or her team. Likewise, two assistant coaches and 10 squad members are standing while the game clock is running and the ball is live. Is this legal?

Ruling: When only one other person is illegally standing, an official shall assess both that individual and the head coach a direct technical foul. When more than one other person is standing, an official shall assess a direct technical foul to the head coach only.

Art. 2. A head coach may leave his or her place on the bench but, in doing so, shall stay within his or her team's coaching box.

Art. 3. Bench personnel shall be permitted to leave the bench area only under the following circumstances:

a. A coach or team attendant may leave the coaching box to seek information from the official scorer or official timer during a timeout or an intermission.

b. A team member may leave the bench area to report to the scorers' table.

c. A coach, squad member or team attendant may leave the bench area at any time to point out a scoring or timing mistake, or to request a timeout to ascertain whether a correctable error needs to be rectified (Rule 2-10).

   1. When there was no mistake on the part of the official scorer or official timer, or the error is not correctable, a timeout shall be charged to the offending team.

d. The head coach may leave the bench area when a fight may break out or has broken out on the playing court.

e. Any team member who leaves the bench area when a fight may break out or has broken out shall be ejected.

   1. No direct technical fouls shall be assessed.

INTERPRETATIONS

Play 1: A6 and B6 leave the bench because a fight has broken out. A6 and B6 do not participate in the fight.

Ruling: A6 and B6 shall be ejected. No free-throw penalties or direct technical fouls shall be assessed to A6 and B6. Because neither participated in the fight, no fighting penalty or suspension shall be invoked against them.

Play 2: A6 and A7 leave the bench because a fight has broken out. A6 and A7 participate in the fight.

Ruling: A6 and A7 shall be ejected immediately upon leaving the bench and entering the playing court. Flagrant technical fouls shall be assessed to A6 and A7 for leaving the bench to participate in a fight. These flagrant technical fouls also shall be assessed to the head coach because A6 and A7 are bench personnel. A6 and A7 shall be subject to the suspension penalty for fighting.

f. Any bench personnel other than the head coach who leaves the bench area when a fight may break out or has broken out shall be ejected.

g. During an intermission or a timeout charged to a team, the coach and/or team attendants may confer with their players at or near the bench within the bench area.

h. In all other circumstances, bench personnel shall remain in the bench area. No part of a foot may touch or be beyond the outer edge of the boundaries of the bench area.

Section 10. Penalty for Infractions of Bench-Area Restrictions

Art. 1. The penalty for infractions of bench-area restrictions is the same as that for any other direct technical foul.

Section 11. Flagrant Technical Fouls

Art. 1. A flagrant technical foul can be either contact or non-contact.

Art. 2. A flagrant non-contact technical foul is an infraction that involves extreme, sometimes persistent, vulgar, abusive conduct.

a. It is a flagrant non-contact technical foul when a player participates after changing his or her uniform number without reporting the change to the official scorer and an official.

b. It is a flagrant non-contact technical foul when a player participates after having been disqualified.

INTERPRETATION

Play: A1, who has been disqualified: (a) reports to the official scorer and is subsequently beckoned onto the playing court by an official; or (b) reports to the official scorer and is beckoned onto the playing court, A1 is not discovered until he or she has participated and scored.

Ruling: Flagrant technical foul in both (a) and (b). A1 shall be ejected and the offended team shall be awarded two free throws and the ball shall be awarded to the offended team. In (b), any score made by A1 shall count. (See Rule 10-11.2.b.)

Art. 3. A flagrant contact technical foul is severely or excessively contacting an opponent when the ball is dead.

Section 12. **Penalty for Flagrant Technical Fouls**

Art. 1. The penalty for a flagrant technical foul shall be two free throws awarded to any member of the offended team and possession of the ball to the offended team at a designated spot at the division line.

Art. 2. The offender(s) shall be ejected.

Art. 3. When a flagrant technical foul is called for fighting, refer to Rule 10-17 for resulting suspension.

Art. 4. A flagrant technical foul shall count toward the team-foul total.

Art. 5. When double flagrant personal fouls are committed, no free throws shall be awarded.

Art. 6. The offenders in a double flagrant foul shall be ejected.

Art. 7. After a double flagrant technical foul, the ball shall be put in play at the point of interruption.

Section 13. **Intentional Technical Fouls**

Art. 1. An intentional technical foul involves intentionally contacting an opponent in a non-flagrant manner when the ball is dead.

Section 14. Penalty for Intentional Technical Fouls

Art. 1. The penalty for an intentional technical foul shall be two free throws awarded to any member of the offended team and possession of the ball to the offended team at the division line.

Art. 2. The offender shall not be ejected.

Art. 3. An intentional technical foul shall count toward a player's five fouls for disqualification and toward the team-foul total.

Art. 4. When double intentional technical fouls are committed, no free throws shall be awarded.

Art. 5. The offenders in a double intentional technical foul shall not be ejected.

Art. 6. After a double intentional technical foul, the ball shall be put in play at the point of interruption.

Section 15. Fighting

Art. 1. Fighting, as defined in Rule 4-23, includes, but is not limited to:

a. An attempt to strike an opponent with the arms, hands, legs or feet.

b. An attempt to punch or kick an opponent, regardless of whether contact is made.

c. An attempt to instigate a fight by committing an unsporting act toward an opponent that causes the opponent to retaliate by fighting.

As determined by the officials, fighting is a flagrant foul and can be either personal (during a live ball) or technical (during a dead ball).

Section 16. Penalty for Fighting/Flagrant Personal Fouls

Art. 1. When fighting occurs during a dead ball, it shall be ruled a flagrant technical foul. (See Rule 10-12 for penalty.)

Art. 2. When fighting occurs during a live ball, it shall be ruled a flagrant personal foul.

Art. 3. For any flagrant personal foul committed by bench personnel, a player or follower, two free throws shall be awarded and the offender shall be ejected.

Art. 4. For any flagrant personal foul, the ball shall be awarded to the offended team at a designated spot.

Art. 5. When double flagrant personal fouls are committed, the offending players shall be ejected, no free throws shall be awarded and the ball shall be put in play at the point of interruption.

Section 17. Suspensions for Fighting

Art. 1. Any member of team personnel who participates in a fight (regardless of whether he or she is a player at the time) shall be assessed a flagrant technical foul.

Art. 2. The first time an individual participates in a fight during the season (including exhibition games), the individual shall be suspended from participating in the team's next regular-season game (not an exhibition contest), including tournament competition.

Art. 3. When an individual participates in a second fight, that individual shall be suspended for the remainder of the season, including tournament competition.

Art. 4. When an individual participates in a fight during his or her team's final game of the season, that individual shall be suspended from participating in the team's next regular-season game (not an exhibition contest) for which that member of team personnel would be eligible.

Art. 5. Any member of team personnel under suspension for fighting shall not be in the team's bench area. (See Appendix I for a summary of fight-reporting procedures.)

Art. 6. The referee may declare a forfeit when any individual fails to comply with any part of the penalties of this Rule.

Art. 7. After a game, conference offices or the assigning authority may correct an error in who was involved in a fight but cannot change an official's ruling that a fight took place or lessen the severity of the penalty. Such entities may make those penalties more severe.

Personal Fouls

Section 18. ## By Players

Art. 1. A player shall not hold, push, charge, trip or impede the progress of an opponent by extending arm(s), shoulder(s), hip(s) or knee(s) or by bending his or her own body into other than a normal position; nor use any unreasonably rough tactics.

Art. 2. A player shall not contact an opponent with his or her hand unless such contact is only with the opponent's hand while it is on the ball and is incidental to an attempt to play the ball.

Art. 3. A player shall not use his or her hand(s) on an opponent to inhibit the freedom of movement of the opponent in any way or to aid an opponent in starting or stopping.

Art. 4. A player shall not extend the arm(s) fully or partially other than vertically so that freedom of movement of an opponent is hindered when contact with the arm(s) occurs.

Art. 5. A player shall not use the forearm and hand to prevent an opponent from attacking the ball during a dribble or when trying for goal.

Art. 6. A player may hold his or her hand(s) and arm(s) in front of his or her own face or body for protection and to absorb force from an imminent charge by an opponent.

Art. 7. Contact caused by a defensive player approaching the player with the ball from behind is pushing; contact caused by the momentum of a player who has tried for goal is charging.

Section 19. **By Dribbler**

Art. 1. A dribbler shall neither charge into nor contact an opponent in the dribbler's path nor attempt to dribble between two opponents or between an opponent and a boundary, unless the space is sufficient to provide a reasonable chance for the dribbler to pass through without contact.

Art. 2. When a dribbler, without contact, passes an opponent sufficiently to have head and shoulders beyond the front of the opponent's torso, the greater responsibility for subsequent contact shall be that of the opponent.

Art. 3. When a dribbler has obtained a straight-line path, the dribbler may not be crowded out of that path; when an opponent is able to legally obtain a defensive position in that path, the dribbler shall avoid contact by changing direction or ending the dribble.

INTERPRETATION

Play: A player who is guarding moves into the path of a dribbler and contact occurs.

Ruling: Either player may be responsible, but the greater responsibility shall be that of the dribbler when the player who is guarding conforms to the following principles that officials shall use in reaching a decision. The defensive player shall be assumed to have attained a guarding position when the defensive player is in the dribbler's path facing him or her. When the defensive player jumps into position, both feet must return to the floor after the jump before he or she can have attained a guarding position. No specific stance or distance shall be required. The guard may shift to maintain his or her position in the path of the dribbler, provided that the player who is guarding does not charge into the dribbler nor otherwise cause contact as outlined in this section. The responsibility of the dribbler for contact shall not shift merely because the player who is guarding turns or ducks to absorb shock when contact caused by the dribbler is imminent. The player who is guarding shall not cause contact by moving under or in front of a passer or thrower after the passer or thrower is in the air with his or her feet off the floor.

Art. 4. The player intending to become the dribbler shall not be permitted additional rights to start a dribble or in executing a jump try for goal, pivot or feint.

Section 20.   By Screener

Art. 1. A player shall not cause contact by setting a screen outside the visual field of a stationary opponent that does not allow this opponent a normal step to move.

Art. 2. A screener shall not make contact with the opponent when setting a screen within the visual field of that opponent.

Art. 3. A screener shall not take a position so close to a moving opponent that this opponent cannot avoid contact by stopping or changing direction.

INTERPRETATION

Play: B1 maneuvers to a position in front of offensive post player A1 to prevent A1 from receiving the ball. A high pass is made out of the reach of B1. The offensive post player A1 moves toward the basket to catch the pass and try for goal. As the pass is made, B2 moves into the path of A1, in a guarding position.

Ruling: This action involves a screening principle. B2 has switched to guard a player who does not have the ball; therefore, the switching player shall assume a position one or two strides in advance of offensive post player A1 (depending upon the speed of movement of A1) to make the action legal. When A1 has control of the ball (provided that the offensive post player A1 is not in the air at the time), the play shall become a guarding situation. When it is a guarding situation involving the player with the ball, time and distance shall be irrelevant.

Art. 4. No player shall set a screen while moving.

Art. 5. When both opponents are moving in exactly the same path and direction and the screener slows down or stops and contact results, the trailing player shall be responsible for such contact.

Art. 6. No player shall use arm(s), hand(s), hip(s) or shoulder(s) to force through a screen or to hold or push the screener.

Art. 7. Screeners shall not line up next to each other within 6 feet of a boundary line and parallel to it so that contact occurs.

a. Screeners shall be permitted to line up parallel to a boundary line and next to each other without locking arms or grasping each other, provided that the screen is set at least 6 feet from that boundary line.

Section 21. Personal-Foul Penalties

Art. 1. The offender shall be charged with a personal foul. When that personal foul is that offender's fifth foul, including any combination of personal fouls, direct technical fouls and intentional technical fouls, the player shall be disqualified.

Art. 2. The offended player shall be awarded free throw(s) as follows:

a. **One free throw for:**

1. A personal foul against a player who attempts a field goal and whose try is successful.

2. Each non-flagrant personal foul that is a part of a multiple personal foul and is not a player-control foul, regardless of whether the offended team is in the bonus.

b. **Two free throws for:**

1. A personal foul against a player who attempts a field goal and whose try is unsuccessful.
2. An intentional personal or flagrant personal foul and the ball awarded at the designated spot.
   a. Any flagrant personal foul shall result in ejection of the offender. The ball shall be awarded to the offended team at a designated spot after the free throws.

INTERPRETATION

Play: One or both foul(s) of either a multiple personal foul or a double personal foul is flagrant.
Ruling: For a multiple personal foul, one free throw shall be awarded for each non-flagrant personal foul and two free throws shall be awarded for the flagrant personal foul. For a double personal foul, no free throws shall be awarded. In either case, any player who commits a flagrant personal foul shall be ejected.

3. (**Women**) A blocking personal foul against the airborne shooter when the basket is missed.
4. Each common foul (except player control), beginning with a team's 10th foul that results from a combination of personal fouls and direct technical fouls during the half.
5. Each flagrant personal foul of a multiple personal foul and the ball awarded to the offended team at a designated spot.
6. A multiple personal foul (unless the offended player attempted a three-point field goal that

was unsuccessful [see Rule 10-21.2.c]) when either personal foul is intentional or flagrant and the ball shall be awarded to the offended team at a designated spot.

c. **Three free throws for:**
A personal foul against a player who attempts a three-point field goal and whose try is unsuccessful. When the personal foul is intentional or flagrant, the ball also shall be awarded to the offended team at the designated spot.

d. **Bonus free throw for:**
Each common foul (except player control) beginning with a team's seventh foul (including personal fouls, direct technical fouls, intentional technical fouls and flagrant technical fouls) during the half, provided that the first attempt is successful.

e. **No free throws for:**
   1. Each common foul before the bonus rule takes effect.
   2. A player-control personal foul.
   3. A double personal foul, even when one or both of the fouls are flagrant or intentional.

f. **In the case of a false double foul or a false multiple foul,** each personal foul shall carry its own penalty. When one of the fouls is a direct or indirect technical foul, the ball shall be put back in play at the point of interruption.

g. **Personal-foul penalty exception:** After the game-clock horn sounds to end the second half or an extra period, only those free throw(s) necessary to determine a winner or whether an(other) extra period is necessary shall be awarded.

INTERPRETATIONS

Play 1: The score is tied when the referee calls a shooting foul on Team B (a) as the game-clock horn sounds simultaneously to end the game or (b) when four seconds remain on the game clock.

Ruling: In (a), the referee shall award two free throws to A1. When A1 makes the first shot, the game shall be over. In (b), A1 shall be awarded two free throws. When A1 makes both free throws, Team B shall be awarded the ball out of bounds at the end line under Team A's basket.

Play 2: Team A is winning, 79-70, when a foul is called against Team B (a) as the game-clock horn sounds simultaneously to end the game or (b) when five seconds remain on the game clock.

Ruling: In (a), no free throws shall be awarded because a winner already has been determined—in this case, Team A. In (b), the free throw(s) shall be awarded because time remains on the game clock.

Section 22. Summary—Administration of Double Fouls

Foul	Penalty	Resumption of Play
Double personal foul	No shots	Award to the team in control. During a throw-in, award to team in possession of ball. (In all other cases, use the alternating-possession arrow.)
Double technical (dead ball)	No shots	Point of interruption
Double personal flagrant (live ball)	No shots, ejection	Point of Interruption
Double flagrant technical	No shots, ejection	Point of interruption

Official
Signals

Official Basketball Signals

START CLOCK

1

Start clock

STOP CLOCK

2
Stop clock

3
Stop clock
for foul

4
WOMEN ONLY
Stop clock for foul using other hand
to point going other direction

5
Stop clock
for jump ball

TIMEOUT

6
WOMEN ONLY
FULL TIMEOUT
Place fingertips & thumbs
of both hands together in
front of chest & spread
hands out to shoulder width

7
ELECTRONIC MEDIA TIMEOUT
Point toward the scorers'
table for radio/TV

SCORER

8
Shorten
timeout for
substitution

9
Two consecutive
30-second
timeouts

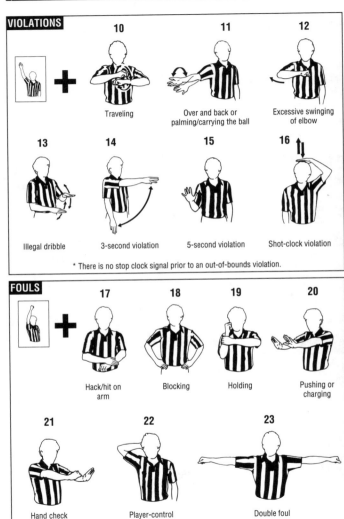

VIOLATIONS

10 Traveling

11 Over and back or palming/carrying the ball

12 Excessive swinging of elbow

13 Illegal dribble

14 3-second violation

15 5-second violation

16 Shot-clock violation

* There is no stop clock signal prior to an out-of-bounds violation.

FOULS

17 Hack/hit on arm

18 Blocking

19 Holding

20 Pushing or charging

21 Hand check

22 Player-control foul

23 Double foul

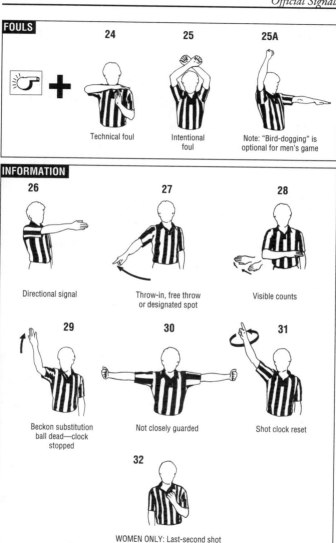

FOULS

24 Technical foul

25 Intentional foul

25A Note: "Bird-dogging" is optional for men's game

INFORMATION

26 Directional signal

27 Throw-in, free throw or designated spot

28 Visible counts

29 Beckon substitution ball dead—clock stopped

30 Not closely guarded

31 Shot clock reset

32 WOMEN ONLY: Last-second shot

SHOOTING

33

No score

34

Goal counts
or is awarded

35

Point(s) awarded
use 1 or 2 fingers
(for 3 points, see No. 36)

36

3-point
field goal

Attempt

and if
successful

37

Bonus free throw
for 2nd throw, drop 1 arm—
for 2 throws use 1 arm with 2 fingers—
for 3 throws use 1 arm with 3 fingers

38

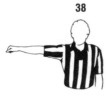

Withheld whistle on a
lane violation by
defensive team

Index
to Rules

Index to Rules